REVIEW FOR THE CLEP* PRINCIPLES OF MANAGEMENT EXAMINATION

Complete review of skills

By
DONALD E. HOVEY, Ph. D.

This book is correlated to the video tapes produced by
COMEX Systems, Inc., Review for The
CLEP* Introduction To Management Examination ©1991
they may be obtained from

comex systems, inc.
5 Cold Hill Road, Suite 24
Mendham, NJ 07945

Published by

comex systems, inc.
5 Cold Hill Road, Suite 24
Mendham, NJ 07945

ISBN 1-56030-145-7

Table of Contents

CLEP* (College Level Examination Program)

CLEP provides a way to determine the level of knowledge you now have in relation to college level material. CLEP does **not** determine your ability to **learn** a subject. People tend to have a **low** evaluation of their ability. There is no way **you** can determine your present level unless **you** take the examination. You can save time and money taking these examinations to earn credit. Others have. Why not YOU?

CLEP INFORMATION

In our reviews, we have found these were the questions most frequently asked by our students:

WHAT IS CLEP?

CLEP is a nation-wide program of testing which began in 1965. Today, over 2,900 colleges recognize CLEP as a way students can earn college credit. Each year over 200,000 persons take CLEP examinations. The testing program is based on the theory that "**what** a person knows is more important than **how** he has learned it." All examinations are designed and scored by the College Entrance Examination Board (CEEB). The purpose of each examination is to determine whether your current knowledge in a subject can qualify you for credit in that area at a particular college.

There are five General Examinations. The topics are:

1. English Composition
2. Mathematics
3. Social Science
4. Natural Science
5. Humanities

Credits earned by achieving on these examinations replace basic liberal arts credits which are required by many colleges for all types of degrees. Each of these general examinations is very broad in coverage. Questions are from the wide range of subjects included in each of the major disciplines. For example, questions in history (ancient, modern, American, European, Black), sociology, psychology, economics and political science could be included on the General CLEP Social Science Examination. The General CLEP Natural Science Examination might include questions related to biology, astronomy, physics, earth science and chemistry. Because of the broad coverage in each examination, you are not expected to be knowledgeable in all areas. There will be some questions on **all** the tests that you will not be able to answer.

There are 29 CLEP Subject Examinations:

HISTORY AND SOCIAL SCIENCES

1. American Government
2. American History I: Early Colonization to 1877
3. American History II: 1865 to Present
4. Introductory Psychology
5. Human Growth and Development
6. Introduction to Educational Psychology
7. Introductory Macroeconomics
8. Introductory Microeconomics
9. Introductory Sociology
10. Western Civilization I: Ancient Near East to 1648
11. Western Civilization II: 1648 to the Present

FOREIGN LANGUAGES

12. College French—Levels 1 and 2
13. College German—Levels 1 and 2
14. College Spanish—Levels 1 and 2

COMPOSITION AND LITERATURE

15. American Literature
16. Analysis and Interpretation of Literature
17. Freshman College Composition
18. English Literature

SCIENCE AND MATHEMATICS

19. Calculus with Elementary Functions
20. College Algebra
21. Trigonometry
22. College Algebra-Trigonometry
23. General Biology
24. General Chemistry

BUSINESS

25. Information Systems and Computer Applications
26. Principles of Management
27. Principles of Accounting
28. Introductory Business Law
29. Principles of Marketing

Each Subject Examination covers material taught in an undergraduate course with a similar title. Questions deal with the specific subject of the examination. Credits earned usually replace those needed for your major.

HOW LONG ARE THE EXAMINATIONS?

Each CLEP General Examination is 1½ hours in length. Each examination is divided into separate timed portions. For a breakdown of each, check with the specific review book for that examination.

Each CLEP Subject Examination is 1½ hours long and is composed of multiple-choice questions to be answered in two separately timed sections. Most Subject Examinations have a 90-minute free-response or essay section which you should take **only** if required by your college.

HOW MUCH DO THE EXAMINATIONS COST?

Currently, the fee to take each examination is $46.00. They may be taken one at a time or in any combination. (NOTE: Fees change periodically.)

WHERE CAN THE EXAMINATIONS BE TAKEN?

The flyers "CLEP COLLEGES" (Listing where you can take the CLEP tests and the colleges that accept credit) and "CLEP INFORMATION FOR CANDIDATES" are available free by calling (609) 771-7865 or writing to: CLEP, PO Box 6600, Princeton, NJ 08541-6600.

There is no charge for these publications. Choose the location which is most convenient to you. The **same** examinations are given at **all** test centers. If you are a member of the armed forces, check with the education officer at your base. Special testings are set up for military personnel.

WHEN ARE THE TESTS GIVEN?

Most CLEP examinations are administered during the third week of every month except December and February. The test center chooses the day of the week. A few test centers administer the tests by appointment only. Check with the center where you will take the test for specific information. If you are serving with the United States Military, check with the Education Services Officer at your base to find out about the DANTES testing program. You will be given information about testing as applicable to military personnel.

HOW DO YOU REGISTER FOR AN EXAMINATION?

A standard registration form can be obtained from the test center where you plan to take the examination. Many centers require that you register (send registration form and fee for examinations to be taken) a month prior to your selected date.

WHEN WILL SCORES BE RECEIVED?

You will receive a copy of your scores approximately six weeks after you take an examination. You can also request that a copy be sent to a college for evaluation. The score you receive will be a scaled score. This score can be correlated to a percentile level. These scores **remain** scores until you become matriculated with a college. CEEB keeps a record of your scores on file for 20 years. You can obtain an additional copy or have a copy sent to a college if you contact:

> College Board
> ATTN: Transcript Service
> PO Box 6600
> Princeton, NJ 08541

Include the date you took the test, the name of the center where you took the test, your date of birth and your social security number. Contact CEEB to find out the current fee for this service.

IS IT NECESSARY TO BE ENROLLED IN A COLLEGE BEFORE YOU TAKE AN EXAMINATION?

That depends. Each college has established policy regarding CLEP. You should check with the school you wish to attend. Many schools do not require that you be enrolled before you take CLEP examinations.

HOW MANY CREDITS CAN BE EARNED?

Each college determines the number of credits that can be earned by achieving on an examination. Most award six credits if you achieve on a CLEP General Examination.

A college usually grants the same amount of credit to students earning satisfactory scores on CLEP Subject Examinations as it grants to students who successfully complete the course.

HOW ARE THE EXAMS SCORED?

See page VII for a detailed explanation of scoring.

HOW ARE THE SCORES EVALUATED?

Before you, a candidate, take an examination, it is administered to college students who are taking a course the examination credits will replace. These students do not take the examination for credit. They take it to establish a standard by which your score can be evaluated. From this testing, percentile levels of achievement can be determined. For example, if you score at the 25th percentile, this would indicate that you achieved as well as the **bottom** 25 percent of those students who took that examination to set a standard.

There is no correlation between the number of questions you answer correctly and the percentile level you achieve. The number would vary from test to test.

CAN THE SAME SCORES EARN A DIFFERENT NUMBER OF CREDITS AT DIFFERENT SCHOOLS?

Yes, because different schools may require different levels of achievement. Your scores may earn you more credit at one institution than at another. For example: if you achieve at the 25th percentile level, you could earn credit at a school which required the 25th percentile level; you could not earn credit at a school which required a higher level of achievement.

CAN CLEP CREDITS BE TRANSFERRED?

Yes, provided the school to which you transfer recognizes CLEP as a way to earn credit. Your scores will be evaluated according to the new school's policy.

CAN AN EXAMINATION BE RETAKEN?

Many schools allow you to retake an examination if you did not achieve the first time. Some do not. Check your particular school's policy before you retake an examination. Also, be **realistic**. If you almost achieved the level at which you could earn credit, do retake the examination. If your score was quite low, take the course it was designed to replace.

IF YOU DECIDE TO RETAKE AN EXAMINATION, six months must elapse before you do so. Scores on tests repeated earlier than six months will be canceled.

HOW CAN I FIND OUT WHAT SCHOOLS ACCEPT CLEP?

In addition to the test centers, there are many other schools that recognize CLEP as a way to earn credit. For a free booklet, CLEP Test Centers and Other Participating Institutions, which lists most of them, send your request, name, and address to:

> The College Board
> Box 6600
> Princeton, NJ 08541

If the school you wish to attend is not listed, call the admissions office at that school and ask for information. Not all participating schools are included in the booklet.

HOW CAN YOU USE THIS BOOK TO IMPROVE YOUR ABILITY?

We recommend the following procedure:

1. Complete the review material. Take the short quizzes which are included with the lessons.

2. If you do well on the sample questions, go on. If you do not, reread the explanatory information.

3. After you have completed the review material, take the sample tests which are in the back of the book. When you take the sample test, try to simulate the test situation as nearly as possible.

   That is:

   a. Find a quiet spot where you will not be disturbed.

   b. Time yourself accurately.

   c. Use the separate answer sheet provided.

   d. When you start the second part of the test, be sure you start to record your answers at the correct number on your answer sheet.

4. Correct the tests. Determine where your weaknesses are. Go back and review those areas in which you had difficulty.

HOW THE EXAMINATIONS ARE SCORED

There is no penalty for wrong answers. Your score is computed based on the number of correct answers. When you are finished with the test, make sure that every question is answered. However, you don't have to answer the question the first time you see it. If you use the coding system, you will greatly increase your score.

THE CODING SYSTEM

Over the years COMEX has perfected a systematic approach to taking a multiple choice examination. This is called the coding system. It is designed to:

1. get you through the examination as quickly as possible.

2. have you answer quickly those questions that are easy for you.

3. have you not waste time on those questions that are too difficult for you.

4. take advantage of all your knowledge of a particular subject. Most people think they can get credit only by knowing an answer is correct. You can also prove your knowledge by knowing an answer is incorrect. The coding system will show you how to accomplish this.

5. get all the help possible by using the recall factor. Because you are going to read the total examination, it is possible that something in question 50 will trigger a thought that will help you answer question 3 the second time you read it.

6. have your questions organized for the second reading so you know what questions offer you the best use of your time.

HERE IS HOW THE CODING SYSTEM WORKS*

We are now going to make you a better test-taker, by showing all of your knowledge and using your time to the greatest advantage. Managing your time on the exam can be as important as knowing the correct answers. If you spend too much time working on difficult questions that you have no knowledge about, you might not get to some easy questions later that you would have gotten correct. This causes a significant decrease in your score. It also makes test taking a very frustrating experience.

Let us attack some sample questions:

1. George Washington was:
    a. the father of King George Washington
    b. the father of Farah Washington
    c. the father of the Washington Laundry
    d. the father of Washington State
    e. the father of our country

As you read the questions you will eliminate all **wrong** answers:

a.	father of King George Washington	NO!
b.	father of Farah Washington	NO!
c.	father of the Washington Laundry	NO!
d.	father of Washington State	NO!
e.	the father of our country	YES. LEAVE IT ALONE.

The question now looks like this:

1.   George Washington was:

~~a.   the father of King George Washington~~
~~b.   the father of Farah Washington~~
~~c.   the father of the Washington Laundry~~
~~d.   the father of Washington State~~
e.   the father of our country

Click on the button next to the correct answer and click next.

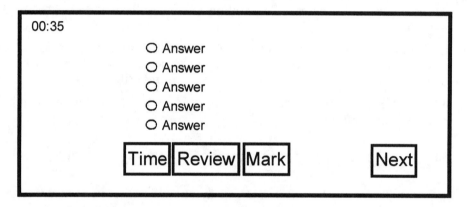

These are the buttons you must know how to use!

You are now finished with this question. Later when we get to the review process, this question will be sorted as answered. This will be your signal to not spend any more time with this question. Any time spent will be wasted.

2.   Abraham Lincoln was responsible for:

a.   freeing the 495 freeway
b.   freeing the slaves
c.   freeing the Lincoln Memorial
d.   freeing the south for industrialization
e.   freeing the Potomac River

Go through the answers.

a.	freeing the 495 freeway	No!
b.	freeing the slaves	Maybe. Always read full question.
c.	freeing the Lincoln Memorial	No!
d.	freeing the south for industrialization	Maybe.
e.	freeing the Potomac River	No!

The question now looks like this:

2. Abraham Lincoln was responsible for:

   a. ~~freeing the 495 freeway~~
   b. freeing the slaves
   c. ~~freeing the Lincoln Memorial~~
   d. freeing the south for industrialization
   e. ~~freeing the Potomac River~~

Should you guess? You have very good odds of getting this question correct. Pick the choice that you feel is the best answer. Often your first guess will be the best. Before clicking the **NEXT** button, click on the **MARK** box. This will tell you later that you were able to eliminate three answers before guessing. Now click on **NEXT** to go on to the next question.

3. Franklin Roosevelt's greatest accomplishment was:

   a. building the Panama Canal
   b. solving the Great Depression
   c. putting America to work
   d. organizing the CCC Corps
   e. instituting the income tax

Go through the answers:

a.	building the Panama Canal	No! That was a different Roosevelt.
b.	solving the Great Depression	Maybe. Go on to the next answer.
c.	putting America to work	Maybe. On to the next answer.
d.	organizing the CCC Corps	Maybe. On to the next answer.
e.	instituting the income tax	Maybe. Leave it alone!

The question now looks like this:

3. Franklin Roosevelt's greatest accomplishment was:

   a. ~~building the Panama Canal~~
   b. solving the Great Depression
   c. putting America to work
   d. organizing the CCC Corps
   e. instituting the income tax

Should you answer this question now? Not yet. There might be a question later that contains information that would help you eliminate more of the answers. When you can only eliminate one answer, or none at all, your best course of action is to simply click on **NEXT**. This will bring up the next question.

Now look at another question:

4.   Casper P. Phudd III was noted for:

    a. rowing a boat
    b. sailing a boat
    c. building a boat
    d. designing a boat
    e. navigating a boat

Even if you have no idea of who Casper P. Phudd III is, read the answers:

a.	rowing a boat	I do not know.
b.	sailing a boat	I do not know.
c.	building a boat	I do not know.
d.	designing a boat	I do not know.
e.	navigating a boat	I do not know.

Since you cannot eliminate any of the answers, simply go on to the next question.

Try another question:

5.   Clarence Q. Jerkwater III

    a. sailed the Atlantic Ocean
    b. drained the Atlantic Ocean
    c. flew over the Atlantic Ocean
    d. colored the Atlantic Ocean orange
    e. swam in the Atlantic Ocean

Even though you know nothing of Clarence Q. Jerkwater III, you read the answers.

a.	sailed the Atlantic Ocean	Possible.
b.	drained the Atlantic Ocean	No way!
c.	flew over the Atlantic Ocean	Maybe.
d.	colored the Atlantic Ocean orange	No way!
e.	swam in the Atlantic Ocean	Maybe.

The question now looks like this:

5.   Clarence Q. Jerkwater III

    a. sailed the Atlantic Ocean
    b. ~~drained the Atlantic Ocean~~
    c. flew over the Atlantic Ocean
    d. ~~colored the Atlantic Ocean orange~~
    e. swam in the Atlantic Ocean

Do you take a guess? Not on the first reading of the answers. Wait to see if the recall factor will help. Do not click on an answer, but do click on **MARK**. Finally, click on next to get the next question.

Continue in this manner until you finish all the questions in the section. By working in this manner you have organized the questions in a way to maximize your efficiency. When you finish with the last question click on **REVIEW**. This brings up the listing of all the questions. They will be listed in numerical order. This in not the way you want to view them. You sorted the questions as you went through them. You want to view the questions sorted. Click on **STATUS**. Now the questions are sorted for you. Let's review what each type means:

Answered without a check mark.
You knew the correct answer.

Answered with a check mark.
You eliminated three answers.

Not answered with a check mark.
You eliminated two answers.

Not answered without a check mark.
You could not eliminate more than one answer.

The Second Time Through

Now you are ready to start your way through the test the second time. Where do you have the best chance of increasing your score? This question should always be at the top of your mind. "How do I show the test evaluators the maximum amount of information I know?" The best place to start is with the questions that you had some idea about, but not enough to answer. These are the questions where you could eliminate two answers. They are marked with a check mark. Clicking on **REVIEW**, and then **STATUS** will sort the questions for you. All of the questions that are marked but have not been answered are grouped together for you.

Click on the first one in the group. Reread the question and the answers. Did anything in any of the other questions give you information to allow you to eliminate any answers? If the answer is yes that is great! The coding system has worked. If you eliminated one more answer make your guess between the remaining two. Leave the **MARK** box checked and click on review to go back to the question list to choose your next question. What if you now know the correct answer? Click on **MARK** to remove the check from the **MARK** box. This question will now be listed as answered. You will not spend any more time on this question. Click on review to go back to your list of questions.

What should you do if you were unable to eliminate any more answers. Now you still need to guess. While your odds are not as good as if you had eliminated three answers, you will have a better chance than if you had eliminated no answers. Any time you eliminate answers before guessing means you arc making an educated guess. Every educated guess you make has a higher chance of being correct than a random guess. More educated guesses means a higher score. Leave the **MARK** box checked. This indicates that you were not sure of your answer.

Continue with this process until you finish all the questions in the group with a check mark that were not answered. Which questions should you work on next? It is now time to work on the questions you had the least knowledge about. These are the questions without a check mark that are not answered. Use the same process that you used for the previous set of questions. Can you now figure out the correct answer? If so, mark it. If not, eliminate as many answers as you can and then choose your best answer. If you guess make sure you check the **MARK** box. Every time you reread a question there is a chance that it will trigger something in your memory that will help you with this question, or with one of the others.

Be very careful to keep track of time. If it is not diplayed at the top of the screen, make sure you click on the box so that it will be displayed. Do not think of the clock as your enemy. It is your friend. It keeps you on your task and moving efficiently through the test.

When you only have five minutes left, go through and make sure that you have every question answered. Remember a blank space counts the same as a wrong answer. If you go through and make an educated guess at all the questions, you will get a better score than if the questions were left blank. Even if you randomly guess you should end up with one correct answer out of every five. Every correct answer will increase your score. If you are guessing, check the **MARK** box so you know you guessed on that question. This will allow you to review that question later if time permits.

Now there are only two types of questions left: questions with correct answers and questions with educated guesses. Does this mean it is time to stop? Not if you want to get the highest possible score. All of the questions with educated guesses have a check mark. Keep working on those problems. Do not waste time looking at any questions that do not have a check.

By using the coding system you will move quickly through the test and make sure that you see every question. It also allows you to concentrate your efforts on your strongest areas.

We purposely used ludicrous questions to emphasize how the system works. Practice the system while you are doing your practice quizzes and tests. You can use a similar system with a piece of scratch paper. Put an "A" next to questions as you answer them. Put a check mark next to a question to refer back to it. Then use the system to go back through the test. The system is easy to master and can be an invaluable tool in your test-taking arsenal.

You have now completed the portion of the book which was designed to improve your test-taking ability. When you work the practice exercises and take the sample test, use these techniques you have just learned.

You can also use the coding system on any other multiple choice test. This will not only increase your score on that test, but it will also make you more comfortable with using the system. It has been demonstrated many times that the more comfortable you are when you are taking a test the higher your score will be.

SOME BASICS FOR THE TEST DAY

1. Get to the examination location early. If you are taking the examination at a new location - check out how to get there **before** the day of the examination.

2. Choose a seat carefully.
   a. In a large room, choose a quiet corner. If possible, sit facing a wall.
   b. If you go with a friend, do not sit together.

3. Stay with your usual routine. If you normally skip breakfast, do so on the test day also, etc.

4. If you do not understand the proctor's directions, ask questions.

5. Do not quit. Keep going over questions you were not able to answer the first time. Beat the examination, do not let it beat you!

6. If you cannot answer a question, code it and go on to the next. Do not spend a lot of time on one question unless you have already finished the rest of that section of the examination. Go through each section and do the easiest questions first, then go back to the difficult ones.

7. **Be sure** you understand the directions for **each** type of test **BEFORE you take the examination**. Not understanding the directions can cause you to lose valuable time when you are taking the actual test.

8. Remember to use the coding system.

9. If you are unfamiliar with how to use a mouse, try to get some practice. Most libraries have computers where you can practice. If you have to learn how to use the mouse at the test site you are putting yourself at a severe disadvantage.

Review for the CLEP Principles of Management
Description of the Examination

This study guide is designed to help you prepare for the CLEP Principles of Management Subject Examination.

The best way to use this review is to go through the material in the order presented, studying the information, completing the exercises, and checking your answers. At the end of the review section there is a short practice examination with explanatory answers. In addition, there is a full-length Principles of Management examination at the end of the book.

The test itself is designed to measure your knowledge of human resources and operational and functional aspects of management with an emp0hasis on the functional aspects.

The Principles of Management Examination is 90-minutes long and includes approximately 100 multiple-choice questions to be answered in two separately timed 45-minute sections.

The content of the examination is approximately as follows:

APPROXIMATE PERCENT OF THE EXAM	TOPIC
20%	Organization an Human Resources Personnel Administration Collective Bargaining Human Relations and Motivation Training & Development Performance Appraisal Organizational Development Effective Communication Legal Concerns Work Force Diversity
15%	Operational Aspects of Management Operations Planning and Control Work Scheduling Quality Management (TQM, e.g.) Information Processing and Management Strategic Planning and Analysis Productivity
50%	Functional Aspects of Management Planning, Organizing, Directing, Controlling, Authority, Decision Making, Organization Charts, Leadership, Organization Structure, Budgeting, Communication, Problem Solving, Group Dynamics, Conflict Resolution, Effective Communication, Change, Organizational Theory
15%	Miscellaneous Aspects of Management Historical Aspects Social Responsibilities of Business Systems International Management and Competition Environment Ethics Government Regulation Management Theory & Theorists

APPROXIMATE PERCENT OF THE EXAM	TOPIC
10%	Specific factual knowledge, recall and general understanding of purposes, functions, and techniques of management.
40%	Understanding of and ability to associate the meaning of specific terminology with important management ideas, processes, techniques, concepts, and elements.
40%	Understanding of theory and significant underlying assumptions, concepts, and limitations of management data, including a comprehension of the rationale of procedures, methods, and analyses.
10%	Application of knowledge, general concepts, and principles to specific problems

Reprinted with permission from The Official Study Guide For the CLEP, copyright © 1982,1987, 1990, 1992, 1994, 1995, 1996 by College Entrance Examination Board, New York.

Chapter 1: Overview

OBJECTIVES: In this chapter you will learn what management is (the functions of management), the management process and major approaches to management. In addition, managerial concerns in the environment of organizations, social responsibilities and international business will be discussed.

Management is figuring out what ought to be done and doing whatever it takes, ethically, to get it done correctly.

There are almost as many definitions of management as authors. Most view management as a process taking place in an organization and consisting of a number of interrelated functions that must be accomplished if the organization is to be effective. (The word **function** means an activity, goal or purpose—something that must be accomplished.)

The **management process** consists of the **functions** of **planning, organizing, staffing, directing** and **controlling**. (Different writers have different numbers of functions in the process and some use different names.)

The **planning function** is concerned with the future. It is the part of the management process in which the organization defines its purpose or mission, establishes its goals, and forecasts the future environments, opportunities, challenges and threats that the organization will have to face. In the planning process alternative courses of action are developed or discovered, decisions are made between alternatives and specific operating and contingency plans are worked out.

The **organizing function** has to do with dividing the work that needs to be done, grouping the human and other resources, establishing a structure of authority and responsibility, and devising means for coordinating the various parts. The irony of organizing is that after you have divided the work to get the benefits of specialization, you have to put it all back together again so that people are pulling for the same goal.

Staffing is the management function, the part of the management process, that puts real people into the organization structure. The other names often used for the staffing function are **personnel management** and **human resources management**. The field of Personnel/Human Resources Management is one of the major subdivisions of the academic discipline of management. (The second major subdivision in the management field is Production/Operations Management.)

The fourth function in the management process is **directing** or **leading** which includes guiding and influencing people to seek organizational objectives.

The last step or function in the management process is **controlling** which is making sure that things are being done in a way that we want. Essentially, **controlling** is the reverse side of planning because in the control function we measure and observe how much actual performance is deviating from plans.

We have used the functions of management as the basis for organizing this book. Chapter Two will discuss planning. In Chapter Three you will learn about organizing. Chapter Four will deal with staffing, Chapter Five with leading or directing. In Chapter Six you will cover the controlling function as well as review some operational considerations in management.

It is sometimes useful to distinguish among the three levels of management: **top management** (or upper management), **middle management**, and **first-line management** (sometimes called lower-level, front-line or supervisory management). In large corporations there will be more than three levels, and in the smallest organizations there may only be two or even one level of management. While there are great differences between individual organizations, industries, and occupations and functional areas, there are some generalizations that can be made about differences between management levels.

One difference has to do with the skills involved and required. Three types of skills involved in managerial work are **technical**, **interpersonal** and **conceptual**. In general, the amount of time and the percentage of the job involved in technical skills is highest for the first-line level of management, somewhat less at middle levels, and smallest at top management level. The diversity of technical skills and knowledge required also changes, but in the opposite way. A top manager must have a working knowledge of a far wider range of technical knowledge than a first-line manager would need. The importance and amount of attention devoted to interpersonal skills seems to remain fairly constant through all management levels. Conceptual skills, which are generally only a fraction of the skills required at lower levels, increase in importance with middle management and become of great importance at top management levels. The ability to think, to plan, to manipulate symbols and concepts is crucial for top management.

Another difference between levels is that only first-line managers supervise non-management people. Middle and top managers supervise other managers.

Professor Henry Mintzberg has identified ten different roles that managers carry out. These give us insight into what managers actually do. Mintzberg divides managerial work into **interpersonal** roles, **informational** roles and **decisional** roles. The various roles underline the part that managers play in promoting the flow of information into, through, and out of the organization, particularly in getting information to where it is needed to make decisions. The **interpersonal** roles include figurehead, leader and liaison; **informational** roles include monitor, disseminator and spokesperson; **decisional** roles are entrepreneur, disturbance handler, resource-allocator and negotiator.

The responsibilities of the various **levels of management** tend to be different. From one point of view, the management process might even be considered distinctive or different for each of these levels. The **first-line** management level has positions such as section head, crew chief, foreman, head nurse, department head. At **middle** management levels are jobs and positions such as district manager, plant manager, base commander, shift superintendent, division director, sales manager. At the **top** of the organization we have the chief executive officer, the president, the vice presidents.

At the top of the organization some of the management functions that tend to be emphasized are planning, particularly the strategic planning function, and organizing. As we move down the organization we find that there is a shift to operational planning, shorter range planning. For first-line management the concern is with execution and things that are happening in the immediate future.

The nature of managerial work varies a great deal with managerial level. There is a great variety of work involved in management no matter what your job. There are many different kinds of jobs that are described as managerial jobs. In fact, the more we know about management, the more varied management work seems to be.

We know that managerial work tends to be highly fragmented and that managers typically are not able to sit for long periods of time. The manager's day tends to be broken into fairly short time increments, 20 minutes or so. Managers deal with many people. American managers, particularly, prefer face-to-face exchange of information rather than reading reports.

INTERNATIONAL MANAGEMENT

One of the things that we become increasingly aware of today is that management is not simply a national, a local or a regional kind of occupation, but it is very much an international phenomenon. Business has become international. We live in a global economy. International business takes many forms. There are traditional ones such as international trade, selling our products in another country, and buying products or materials abroad. We hear about **multi-national firms (MNF's)** or multi-national corporations **(MNC's)**; these words essentially refer to the same thing.

The typical or model multi-national corporation would be one such as Philips, a Dutch multi-national corporation that has its world headquarters in Eindhoven, The Netherlands. It has component companies set up to operate essentially autonomously, somewhat independent of the parent company, in different countries all over the world: in the United States, in Malaysia, in England and so forth. All of these national companies operate under the general overall guidance and supervision of the parent company at home. This makes it a multi-national company.

Another type of company is the so-called **global company** which is usually a name given to a company that specializes in a single product—such as Coca-Cola was at one time in its history or an oil company. A global company deals with a single product that is sold in many different countries all over the world.

Other forms of international business can include **direct investment**, for example, the building of a hotel in another country or **portfolio investment**, buying stock in companies from other countries.

Perhaps the most important thing to bear in mind in the area of international management is the importance of cultural differences. Anyone who is involved in any way in management overseas needs to be aware of the fact that people from different cultures have different attitudes, different values, different things that are important to them; these differences affect their work, and also influence the management process. In fact, one of the things we need to know more about is whether management as a process is something that is generic—the same sort of thing all over the world—or whether there are culturally distinct and different forms of management: Japanese management, North American management and so on.

ENVIRONMENT OF ORGANIZATIONS

The awareness of society and the role that it frequently plays in the background for business and other organizational activities brings us to another area that we need to be aware of: the environment.

This is an area that is frequently at the forefront of attention of top management because of their role as planners and also because they actively attempt to influence the environment. Organizational environment refers to business-and-society relationships in particular. One aspect of the environment of organizations, particularly the environment of business, that we need to be very conscious of is the legal environment. In the United States and many other Western countries, in particular, we have a structure of laws that is not only extremely supportive of business activity, but without which business activity as we know it would not be possible.

One example would be the concept of the **corporation**. The corporation is a fiction. It is something that is made up by our imagination according to the law. The law permits us to pretend that this thing we call the corporation is a real human being that has the rights of a human being. It can enter into contracts, collect debts and do any number of things that people can do. It is protected by the laws just as people are. However, it has one incredible advantage that people do not have: it is immortal. It goes on forever, it does not die and go out of existence. That is one of the advantages of the corporation as a form of business organization when it is compared to the form of partnership. A partnership ceases to exist with the death of a partner.

One very important notion in this whole area of business and society and the environment of business, is the idea of **legitimacy**. Society permits organizations to exist only to the extent that they provide some kind of useful function that society recognizes as legitimate or acceptable. Most organizations want to make sure that the society or the opinion leaders of their society think of their organization as being valuable to the society. They want to be useful and to accomplish worthwhile purposes. This is accomplished in part through public relations activities and also by other representational or figurehead kinds of activities on the part of the organization's top management. The organization also attempts to influence the environment, particularly the government, to make the environment more supportive and helpful to the organization. As part of this concept of legitimacy we expect the organization leaders to not only observe the law—be very conscious of it—and make sure that the people in their organization are aware of and observe legal requirements, but we also expect more than this. We expect organizations to have a sense of **social responsibility**. We expect them to have a **sense of ethics**, ideas of what is right and equitable and fair, in addition to simply whether it is legal or not. The most respected organizations are the ones that behave in an ethical manner.

Most large organizations have a code of ethics. The organizations that are the most effective tend to pay a lot of attention to making sure that the code of ethics is made available to employees, and that top managers serve as role models in ethical behavior. The organization invests in structures, processes, and procedures to insure that ethical procedures are followed by members of the organization.

A final perspective that is very useful in thinking about the environment of the organization is the **stakeholder** perspective. While helpful to those at the top of the organization who are making policy and developing organizational strategy, it is also a perspective that is important for everybody to be aware of. A stakeholder is anyone who can affect the organization or who can be affected by it. A stakeholder is anyone who is concerned about how the organization does its business. Obviously, some of those people who are concerned would include stockholders (the owners of the organization), the managers of the organization, and other employees. Outside the formal boundaries of the organization, but still very much involved with it, are customers, suppliers, governments, competitors, the community in which the organization exists and society as a whole. It is important to assess the role that each of these stakeholder groups can play in contributing to the success or the lack of success of any organizational course of action.

PERSPECTIVES ON MANAGEMENT

There are five perspectives on the management process that we are going to touch upon. You can think of them as historical perspectives because they certainly had their starting point sometime in the history of management. However, that is not really why we are interested in them. Most managers and writers of management textbooks are not very interested in history for its own sake. They are interested in these historical perspectives, not because they are historical, but because they are current and alive and very much with us today. We see these in operation in many of the approaches that people take to organizational problems.

One of the hallmarks of current management is called the **contingency approach**. This is the idea that there is not necessarily one best way of managing that is suitable for every situation. Instead the situation or problem should be analyzed. We should then come up with the management approach or combination of approaches that is going to be most effective and appropriate for our particular situation. In doing this, we can identify managers drawing on these different perspectives or ways of doing things. Some approaches have a long history in management thinking.

SCIENTIFIC MANAGEMENT

The oldest approach of them all, particularly in the United States, is **Scientific Management**. Scientific Management is associated with Frederick Winslow Taylor, an engineer who originally was with Midvale Steel. He later worked at Bethlehem Steel. Some other names that you will hear in connection with Scientific Management are: Henry L. Gantt, who we will meet later when we talk about scheduling and production management because he developed the Gantt Chart which is very useful for scheduling; and Frank and Lilian Gilbreth, who were described in the book and motion picture Cheaper by the Dozen.

Frank Gilbreth believed in finding the one best way of doing any job. He used time and motion studies extensively. He sincerely believed that by careful systematic scientific analysis you could determine the best, most efficient, fastest, and easiest way to do any job (e.g., laying bricks). That illustrates an important aspect of Scientific Management which is that it tends to focus on manual work to be done at the job level. In the different levels of management that we talked about, this would be the concern particularly of first-line management, the managers who are supervising the work. Middle level managers who are working out the procedures by which the work is to be done would also be interested. Scientific Management was not involved with broad and all-encompassing organizational issues.

Scientific Management had four main ideas or principles that it was associated with. The **first** principle, the **scientific study of work**, was the type with which Frank Gilbreth and Frederick Taylor were associated. It involved using systematic scientific procedures, measurements, timing, and careful objective observation of the work; gathering information about how the work could be done most efficiently; and establishing that method of performing it. The **second** principle was **selecting** the workers systematically and scientifically for the work to be done. **Third** was **training** the workers in the methods developed by Scientific Management, providing them with **incentives** for working in the way that had been established as best and giving them enthusiastic and cooperative leadership support. The **fourth**, and final point—very important—was the idea that the **work** would no longer simply be turned over to a journeyman to figure out how to do it, but that it would be **divided** between management and the workers. The managers would do the analysis and the planning, figure out how the work should be done, do the setups and the scheduling. The workers would do the manual work itself, essentially doing what they were told. Of course, much criticism has come to that approach because it means de-skilling the workers and de-skilling the jobs so that the jobs people are doing are no longer as interesting; they may be so elementary that they are absolutely boring. The ultimate example was probably Henry Ford's application of some of the approaches to Scientific Management.

One of Ford's ideas was that the man who put the nut on the bolt on cars going down the assembly line would not tighten it. He reasoned that by the time the man had put on the nut that the wheel would have moved down the assembly line and another man could tighten it. You can imagine what a job is like that consists of simply putting nuts onto bolts and leaving them to be tightened by someone else. Obviously, it would be a pretty mindless job; but that is the negative end of some of the applications of Scientific Management.

CLASSICAL APPROACH

The second major perspective we need to look at is the **Classical Management** approach. This is sometimes called **administrative management**. It features a Frenchman named Henri Fayol who is sometimes called the "father of modern management." Fayol was the head of a large French industrial and mining organization. He wrote about management in a fairly thin volume that is still worth reading today.

Fayol was the first to identify management as a distinct and separate activity. In his view, management was something over and above the commercial, the accounting, and the technical sides of the business. Fayol was the one to first distinguish the **functions of management** which he listed as planning, organizing, commanding, coordinating and controlling. As I have indicated earlier, every writer has his own list of management functions; some authorities have as many as ten different functions; everybody has at least these three—planning, organizing and controlling.

Fayol also developed **14 principles of management**. These were general guidelines, dealing particularly with the function of commanding. It was believed if you studied these ideas and applied them properly you would be able to do an effective job of running an organization. Fayol's principles included division of labor, the idea that authority should be equal to responsibility, unity of command, unity of direction, need of equitable pay, centralization, chain of command—that he called the Scalar Chain—initiative and *esprit de corps*. We see, even today, that many of Fayol's ideas are still with us, particularly: that responsibility has to be equal to authority; unity of command, the idea that no employee should have more than one person telling him what to do; unity of direction, that for any goal or objective that the organization has there should be only one overall plan for getting there and there should be one person in charge, not everybody doing his own thing. These are important ideas and they are still practiced today.

HUMAN RELATIONS

The third major perspective from a historical point of view is **human relations**, sometimes called the **behavioral** perspective.

The human relations perspective is associated with a famous set of studies called the **Hawthorne Studies**. These were conducted by and at the Western Electric Company Hawthorne plant in Cicero, Illinois (a suburb of Chicago). The management theorists who are associated with this work and with the start of the **human relations movement** are Elton Mayo and Fritz Roethlisberger, both of the Harvard Business School. The Hawthorne Studies are ones that you will constantly hear about as you go through the management curriculum. They are probably the most extensive and long-term set of systematic investigations ever conducted in the field of management. They started in the mid 1920's and ran to the beginning of World War II.

The first part of the Hawthorne Studies, called the Illumination Studies, went on for several years and was conducted in the spirit of Scientific Management. It involved attempting to determine the exact amount of illumination that was best for doing any particular kind of work. As the intensity of the illumination was increased, the work output also increased. And then, being good researchers, they started to reduce the illumination and found that production still increased. In fact, they had several workers claim that the ideal illumination was about the intensity of moonlight. This fact that performance improves simply because you are investigating it became known as the Hawthorne Effect. In the case of the Hawthorne Studies, it also led researchers to realize that something else was happening. It could be just the attention the workers were getting, but it needed to be investigated more completely. At that point, the people from Harvard were brought in to look at some of the other things that were in the Scientific Management tradition including rest pauses, the amount of food that the people were fed, snacks, humidity in the room, and so on.

The key part of the Hawthorne Studies was the relay assembly room study that involved half-a-dozen women assembling telephone relay equipment. Over a period of two or three years production had gradually increased no matter what changes were made. Production reached a point where it was about 33 percent higher than it had been to start. The researchers then took away all the changes that had been put into the system. The production level stayed constant, 33 percent higher!

Again, the Hawthorne Effect was one possible explanation. From that study and other parts of the Hawthorne Studies, Roethlisberger and Mayo concluded that what was happening was not just the effect of the Scientific Management kinds of changes: rest pauses, working conditions, physical conditions and so on. Also important were the effects of psychological and social factors: the understanding leadership, the participative kind of atmosphere in which the employees' opinions about changes and working conditions were sought, the recognition of the importance of group norms and the informal organization. They believed that all of these were involved in the improvement of output. This indicates that morale was as important as physical conditions. This then became the basis of the human relations movement that was concerned with improving things like morale, communication, leadership, and relations between supervisor and employees. Roethlisberger and Mayo saw the factory as a social system, and they emphasized that you need to understand the social system just as much as the technological and the engineering side of the operation if you are going to be successful.

BUREAUCRACY

The next approach which we need to understand is the **bureaucracy theory** as developed by Max Weber, a great German sociologist. Max Weber described the kind of organization that we see today in many governmental forms. More importantly, the modern efficient business organization would fit very much into Weber's model of bureaucracy.

Weber distinguished among **three kinds of authority**. There was **traditional authority**: one followed orders and gave respect to someone simply because that was the way you had been brought up; or he was the king or the noble and that was what you were supposed to do; or he was the owner of the family business or the son of the owner, so because of tradition you did what that individual told you to. The basis of this person's authority is traditional authority.

Another kind of authority that Weber talked about was **charismatic authority**: the leader is followed because of the magnetism, the charm, the respect, the admiration, or even reverence that he engenders in people. We see this to some extent in all politicians and to a great extent in a few politicians and unusual leaders. In an extreme form, the followers see the leader as a holy person, maybe even as a prophet or a god. Following that person's dictates is a religious kind of obligation.

The third authority that you have with a bureaucracy and in the modern organization is one Weber called **rational-legal authority**. This is the basis of bureaucracy. A bureaucracy is a system of jurisdictions in which authority and responsibility are carefully specified. There is specialization. People are recruited to the organization and assigned to jobs based not on who they know or who their relatives are, but on the basis of expertise, training, experience, and examinations. There is a hierarchy of authority in which the work of any one level of the organization is supervised by specific, identified superiors at the next level of the organization.

In the bureaucracy there is a career orientation. The members of the organization tend to be professionals with lifetime tenure. The organization is expected to be their sole and full-time means of employment. There is a distinction between the property of the individual and the property of the organization. The individual cannot take his job in the organization as something that he owns, that he can pass on to his children, or give away to his relatives and friends. His property is separate from the property of the organization. The organization works on the basis of written records and rules and has formal procedures. These rules provide protection and equity both for the clients of the organization and for the employees of the organization. The employee of the organization cannot be dismissed without cause and the client's claim cannot be refused without reason. So the organization does its business, treats its members, and its clients, on the basis of objectivity and rules—it is impersonal. Things are not done subjectively on the basis of how I feel about you, but on the basis of I do what I do because there is a rule that says I should do it that way.

Weber felt, and there are other management theorists today who share the view—Charles Perrow for instance—that bureaucracy is the most powerful and efficient form of organization that has ever been developed, despite all of its dysfunctional consequences. We are all familiar with the frustrations, the delays and so forth, that bureaucracies can bring. Despite that, it is seen as a very efficient way of doing business. One of the problems with bureaucracy as a form of organization is that it tends to assume that all of the problems and possibilities that will have to be dealt with in the future have been foreseen already in the organization's rules and procedures. And, of course, if things are changing very rapidly and there are new, unheard of and unthought of problems that are confronting the organization, the bureaucracy is not going to be very effective in trying to deal with them.

SYSTEMS APPROACH

A final perspective that we should examine is the **systems approach** or systems theory. This is the idea that you have to look at an organization in terms of parts, or sub-systems, all of which interact with one another. An important idea in systems theory is the distinction between **open systems** and **closed systems**. A closed system is one that you can analyze as though it is in a black box with rigid and impenetrable boundaries that seal it off from the rest of the world.

Systems theorists tend to be open systems people who think like the famous management theorist, Chester Barnard. They believe that you need to look at organizations as being very much in interaction with the environment around them. Chester Barnard, as president of the New Jersey Bell Telephone Company, viewed the organization as including not just its employees, but he also saw the organization as a system that included customers, suppliers, and other people who affect and were affected by the organization. This is open systems thinking.

The systems approach tends to take organizational problems, move them to very high levels of abstraction to look at relationships at that level, and then move back to reality with new connections that could not be seen otherwise. At the extreme, it sees organizations as **systems** of **inputs**, **transformations**, and **outputs**. The organization brings in people and materials from the outer environment, it performs some kind of transformation process on those things—either intentionally or unintentionally—and then it discharges outputs/products into the environment. Most of the output is perhaps intentional, but some, pollution and so on, are unintentional. We then have a **feedback** coming back and affecting the input process.

The idea that everything affects everything else is particularly important when you are planning. You need to recognize that you cannot change one part of the organization without that change having an impact on other parts.

8

CONTINGENCY APPROACH

All of these different approaches to management get drawn on by the **contingency approach**, which is that there is no one best way. We need to diagnose each situation to find the approach that is most appropriate for that situation. The focus is on finding the important dimensions that can be used to analyze situations and prescribe the best management medicine.

NAMES TO REMEMBER:

Chester Barnard   - Saw organization as open system

Henri Fayol   - Classical Approach, Functions of Management, 14 Principles of Management, "Father of Modern Management"

Henry L. Gantt   - Scientific Management, Gantt Charts for Scheduling

Frank and Lilian Gilbreth   - Scientific Management, "One Best Way", Science of Bricklaying

Elton Mayo   - Hawthorne Studies, Human Relations Movement, Behavioral Approach

Henry Mintzberg   - Managerial Roles—Interpersonal, Informational, Decisional

Fritz Roethlisberger   - Hawthorne Studies, Behavioral Approach, Human Relations

Frederick W. Taylor   - "Father of Scientific Management"

Max Weber   - Bureaucracy Theory

KEY WORDS, PHRASES, AND ABBREVIATIONS:

(write out definitions and examples below)

behavioral approach

bureaucracy

classical approach/theory

closed systems

conceptual skills

contingency approach

controlling (function), control

decisional (managerial) roles

direct investment

directing (function)

environment of management/organizations

first line management

functions of management

Hawthorne Studies

human relations movement/approach

Human Resources Management

informational roles

inputs

international business/management

interpersonal skills

leading (function)

middle management

management

management functions

management process

managerial roles

multi-national corporation (MNC)/multi-national firm (MNF)

organizing (function)

open systems

outputs

personnel management

planning (function)

portfolio investment

principles of management

Scientific Management

staffing (function)

stakeholders/stakeholder approach

social responsibilities

Systems Approach

technical skill

top management

traditional management

transformation process

upper level management

Chapter 1: Sample Questions

1. The basic functions of management are:

    (A) planning, organizing, staffing (Human Resources Management), directing or leading, controlling
    (B) finance, production, marketing, personnel
    (C) line and staff
    (D) management and labor
    (E) none of the above

2. The management function that is concerned with division of work and relationships between people is:

    (A) planning
    (B) organizing
    (C) staffing
    (D) directing
    (E) controlling

3. Almost all authorities would include which of the following in their list of FUNCTIONS of management?

    (A) authorizing
    (B) scheduling
    (C) prioritizing
    (D) controlling
    (E) thinking

4. The management functions include some or all of the following:

    (A) planning, directing, controlling
    (B) assets, liabilities, equity
    (C) purchasing, warehousing, sales credit
    (D) forecasting, goal-setting, decision-making
    (E) bargaining, contracting, delivering

5. Which of the following is NOT one of the functions of management:

    (A) organizing
    (B) staffing
    (C) directing
    (D) computing
    (E) planning

6. Management was defined as a:

    (A) function
    (B) right
    (C) process
    (D) responsibility
    (E) fantasy

7. The management process consists of:

(A) fair treatment of all
(B) the functions of planning, organizing, staffing, directing, and controlling
(C) the principles of hierarchy, unity of command, and span of control
(D) the managerial roles of figurehead, monitor, and decision-maker
(E) doing, profiting, accounting

8. Time-and-motion studies and the attempt to find the "one best way" to perform manual work are associated with:

(A) human relations
(B) the systems approach
(C) the contingency approach
(D) scientific management
(E) none of the above

9. Which of the following is NOT a principle of Scientific Management:

(A) job enrichment
(B) systematically establish a body of valid knowledge about each job
(C) select workers rationally on the basis of skills, abilities and attitudes
(D) teach workers how best to do the job and provide incentives for doing it that way
(E) none of the above are exceptions

10. The characteristics of bureaucracy as an organizational form or system are described (set forth by):

(A) Sigmund Freud
(B) Max Weber
(C) Henri Fayol
(D) Fritz Roethlisberger
(E) C. McCarthy

11. The Hawthorne Studies are associated with:

(A) the behavioral or human relations approach to management
(B) Scientific Management
(C) Classical Management
(D) the systems approach
(E) contingency approach

12. The Hawthorne Studies were conducted:

(A) at the Western Electric Co. Hawthorne plant near Chicago, IL
(B) by Henry Hawthorne
(C) during World War II
(D) in the Hawthorne forests of England
(E) at Malibu Beach

13. The Hawthorne Studies are a landmark event in which of the following approaches to management:

   (A) Scientific Management
   (B) managerial process school
   (C) behavioral approach
   (D) classical approach
   (E) contingency approach

14. What best approach to management do these statements suggest?

   "Everything affects everything else" and "Organizations receive inputs from the environment and transform them into outputs to that environment."

   (A) the contingency approach
   (B) the Scientific Management approach
   (C) the behavioral approach
   (D) the systems approach
   (E) none of the above

15. The idea that there is NOT one best way to manage which applies to all situations characterizes the:

   (A) systems approach
   (B) classical approach
   (C) behavioral approach
   (D) traditional approach
   (E) contingency approach

16. The organization's stakeholders would NOT include which of the following:

   (A) stockholders
   (B) employers
   (C) customers
   (D) buildings and equipment
   (E) managers

17. A company which has world headquarters in The Netherlands and separate subsidiaries which operate as semi-autonomous businesses in a variety of other countries, is often referred to as a(an):

   (A) captive company
   (B) corporation
   (C) multi-national corporation (MNC)
   (D) international trading company
   (E) functional organization

Chapter 1: Answers

1.   A   The functions of management are planning, organizing, staffing, directing, and controlling.

2.   B   The management function that divides work and relationships between people is organizing.

3.   D   Controlling—see #1 above.

4.   A   See answer to #1 above.

5.   D   See answer to #1 above. "Computing" is NOT one of the functions of management.

6.   C   Management is a process.

7.   B   We can not repeat this list too often. It is also the basis on which this text has been organized.

8.   D   Scientific Management—especially Frank Gilbreth asserted that for any task one could scientifically determine the one best way to perform it.

9.   A   Job enrichment was not a principle of Scientific Management—B, C, and D are.

10.   B   Max Weber

11.   A   The Hawthorne Studies were concerned with the human relations approach to management.

12.   A   The Hawthorne Studies were conducted starting in 1924 at the Hawthorne Plant of the Western Electric Co. in Cicero, IL (a suburb of Chicago).

13.   C   The Hawthorne Studies mark the advent of the behavioral approach to management—sometimes known as the Human Relations Movement.

14.   D   The systems approach.

15.   E   The contingency approach.

16.   D   Stakeholders are groups of *people* interested in or affected by the organization's actions. Buildings and equipment are not people.

17.   C   This is a typical description of a multi-national Corporation (MNC or MNF).

Chapter 2: Planning

Planning is the management function that deals with the future–what it will be like, what goals will have to be reached, how to reach those goals. According to a classical principle of management known as the **primacy of planning**, planning has to occur before the other management functions can take place.

The **planning process** consists of forecasting the future environment; clarifying or envisioning the mission of the organization; establishing goals; identifying and understanding problems and finding solutions/alternative courses of action/strategies; deciding between alternatives; developing operational plans; planning for contingencies; and finally, reviewing the plans and the planning process.

The concept of the **hierarchy of plans** is that planning flows in a top-down sequence from an overall vision of where the enterprise is going and how to get there, to successively more specific, focused and detailed levels of plans, such as from mission to strategic (long-range plans) to operational (short-term plans).

The mission or **mission statement** gives the overall role or purpose of the organization. It is usually the start of the planning process and at the top of the hierarchy of plans.

Next in the planning process is goals. **Goals** are the desired end states which should be attained in order for the organization to carry out its mission.

The famous management writer Peter Drucker has urged that every enterprise, both public and private, profit and nonprofit, have objectives in each of eight **Key Results Areas**. These are market share, productivity, profitability, innovation, resources (both physical and financial), worker performance and morale, manager performance and development and social responsibilities.

Market share is the enterprise's proportion or percentage of total sales in a region, country, or the world.

Productivity is output divided by input; its determinants include efficiency of labor, technology and capital and, perhaps most important, the competence of management.

Profitability is defined broadly–going beyond dollars–as the benefit resulting from an activity.

Innovation is the introduction of things that are new–technology, methods, ideas and, most important, new products and services.

Resources include capital, the physical plant and equipment.

Worker performance and morale contribute to productivity, product quality, and the reputation of the organization not only for its goods and services but also as a place to work.

Manager performance and development deal with perhaps the most critical aspects of the firm–the quality of its management and the continuous availability and updating of managerial competence.

Social responsibilities generally include the obligation to perform the organization's primary function (for example, make a profit, prevent an enemy from attacking), but to do so in a way that does not have harmful side effects to society. A pro-active view of social responsibilities sees obligations to benefit society that go beyond the primary mission of the organization.

Another checklist approach to planning is **WOTS-UP analysis.** The initials stand for weaknesses, opportunities, threats and strengths underlying planning.

Strategic planning or long-range planning follows goals in the planning hierarchy. A **strategy** is a broad conception of how to achieve the organization's goals. In a narrower sense, it is also used to mean an option or alternative course of action in a decision situation.

Long-range plans generally refer to those covering a period of more than one year into the future. Each organization, however, must define **long-range** and **short-range** on the basis of its own situation; there is no standard time frame for long-range. The terms **strategic planning** and **long-range planning** are often used synonymously and are considered a primary responsibility of top management (assisted by staff).

Operational planning (also called **action planning**) provides the detailed plans and assignments of responsibilities and authority required to execute strategic plans. As details of organization and execution develop, we see the merging of the planning function into the functions of organizing, staffing, and directing.

The term **responsibility** will appear again when we discuss organizing. It is an obligation to complete a task or achieve some goal. In operational and action planning, responsibilities for specific actions and objectives must be assigned.

Objectives are results, attainments, or accomplishments used as the end points for plans and actions. The term **objective** is usually (but not always) used in a narrower, more time-limited and more operational sense than goal.

Management by Objectives (MBO) brings the planning process down to the individual. In its most general meaning MBO is the idea often attributed to Peter Drucker of judging and controlling employee performance on the basis of results rather than by telling him or her what to do every step of the way. MBO is also a system of performance planning and appraisal (control) in which the subordinate (with some guidance from the superior) develops a limited number of specific measurable objectives to be achieved that quarter or year. The subordinate's performance is then evaluated on the basis of how well he/she achieves the objectives.

TYPES OF PLANS

Plans can also be divided into two main categories of **standing** and **single-use**.

Standing plans are those that are always in effect. They include **policies, procedures, and rules**.

A **policy** is a type of standing plan which guides thinking, problem-solving and decision-making. At the overall organizational level they are similar to strategies.

Procedures provide step-by-step guides to action, thinking or decision. Examples are an aircraft pilot's preflight checklist or the loan application procedure of a bank.

A **rule** is a type of standing plan which prescribes (or prohibits) behavior in usually specific terms. For example: "Always thank the customer for the purchase," or "Keep off the grass."

Single-use plans are those intended for a specific, one-time purpose or to cover a fixed time period. They include **programs, projects and budgets**.

> **Programs** are usually broad and fairly long-term, often covering a specified time period. They bring together a variety of actions and organizations (or their representatives) for the attainment of a common goal, such as putting a man on the moon or opening a market for umbrellas in Greenland.

> **Projects** are usually of shorter time span and are more narrowly focused than programs. They could be components of a program. Typically, they bring together people from different parts of the organization to accomplish some task, such as moving the furniture and files from the old office building to the new one or organizing the annual company picnic.

> A **budget** is a plan for the use of resources (usually along with expected results) stated in quantitative (e.g., monetary) terms. Budgets are usually for specific time periods, such as one year.

A variant of single-use plans is a **rolling plan**. It usually involves a long-range plan that is updated at regular intervals (e.g., yearly) and extended into the future for the specified period. For example, a five-year plan is revised each year and extended five years into the future.

Contingency plans are perhaps best thought of as part of the operational planning process. Contingency planning involves expecting the unexpected. You determine what could go wrong or the improbable event that could happen (e.g., rain on your parade, a flat tire, or fire). Contingency planning addresses how to reduce the likelihood of the contingencies and how to deal with them if they occur.

FORECASTING; PLANNING PREMISES

A first or early step in the planning process is **forecasting**, establishing the premises or assumptions on which plans will be based. A large number of forecasting techniques exist. Areas of special interest are economic, technological, social-cultural, and sales or demand. The term **premises of planning** refers to forecasts about the future environment which serve as the assumptions on which planning is based.

Economic forecasting uses a variety of methods to predict general levels of economic activity for a locality, region, country or the whole world. One approach to economic forecasting uses economic indicators such as unemployment figures and bank interest rates on loans. Leading indicators also include Standard and Poor's index of stock prices, new orders for durable goods and new building permits. These tend to lead or foretell ups and downs in overall economic activity. Econometric models are used in forecasting too, particularly to predict the impact of one particular change or contingency on the overall economy. If you have a good model of how the economy of a particular metropolitan area works, for example, you can ask many "what if?" questions: what would be the impact of increased property taxes? of a new manufacturing plant?

Technological forecasting is predicting the state of scientific and technological knowledge and the kind of machinery and skills that will exist. One kind of forecast involves continuing existing trends out into the future and describing their implications. Another approach is to ask what kind of technological developments would be required to achieve some specific goal at a specified future date (e.g., to establish a permanent colony on the moon by the year 2001).

There are many approaches to technological forecasting. One that has had some popularity is called the **Delphi Method** and is used mainly with expert respondents in the field of interest. The method was perfected at the RAND Corporation, a think tank. It is a method of getting a collection of individuals to state their judgments, review them, and then make a final judgment about some question. Respondents never interact directly with one another; they submit anonymous opinions or estimates to a central point where the opinions are summarized and reported back to the respondents. The respondents are then asked to make a revised estimate. The process is repeated until a consensus is approached.

Sales forecasting, broadly defined, includes the predicted demand for the goods or services provided by the organization. In this sense, **sales forecasts** are of vital importance for operational and production planning. A number of sales forecasting methods are available–some of them are quite sophisticated.

One traditional method of sales forecasting has been **expert opinion,** sometimes called jury of executive opinion. It consists of asking marketing executives what they expect will happen. It can be used to forecast anything (not always correctly).

Another sales forecasting method, which asks the customers what they think, is **market research**. It employs several techniques which can lead to forecasts of consumer tastes, likelihood of product acceptance, and sales or demand. It involves asking people questions about what they like and dislike and what they expect to do.

A number of **statistical methods** have been used in sales forecasting. One technique is the use of regression analysis, or correlations between variables, to predict one from the other–for example, to predict housing starts from marriages.

PROBLEM-SOLVING AND DECISION-MAKING

Decision-making is the name given to the next part of the planning process. In our view it consists of two main parts: problem-solving and decision-making. Nobel Prize winner Herbert Simon viewed management as decision-making and involving **three phases: intelligence, design** and **choice**. The intelligence phase involves intelligence in the sense of gathering knowledge which leads to an understanding of what decisions will have to be made and the general nature of the problems facing the organization. In the design phase alternative courses of action to deal with problems or opportunities are invented or discovered and decision criteria is specified. Finally, in the choice phase the actual decision or choice between alternatives is made.

Which ever approach is taken, **decision-making involves** at minimum **a choice** between two or more alternatives. Many quantitative methods exist to assist in decision-making. (Some of these are discussed under Operations Research Methods in Chapter Six.)

Problem-solving is that part of the planning process in which problems are defined, understanding of cause-and-effect relationships is acquired, and alternative courses of action or problem solutions are identified or generated. It precedes decision-making and is included as part of it by many authors. In general, the more solutions or alternatives one has to choose from, the more likely a good solution will be chosen.

Generating ideas and solutions involves different psychological processes from the criticism and evaluation which must be part of decision-making. For this reason **brainstorming** was invented to keep the two processes, idea generation and idea evaluation, separate. Brainstorming is a technique of creative problem-solving most often used to generate alternatives. The rules are: no criticism; the crazier the ideas the better (free wheeling); the more ideas the better; build on ideas which others have stated (piggyback); and postpone all evaluation until all ideas have been presented. Although brainstorming is a popular method, research suggests that from the same number of persons working alone you will get more ideas.

The **steps in problem-solving and decision-making** are: define the problem; analyze information and try to understand cause-and-effect relations; generate alternative solutions; identify criteria; make the decision using the criteria; develop action and contingency plans.

There are two kinds of **decision criteria:** musts and NTH's ("nice to have's"). Criteria can include attributes such as the number of square feet in a factory, the number of bedrooms in a house; they can be limits such as maximum monthly payment or down payment on a house; they can be objectives like "generates $50,000 in rents per year" or "seats 100 diners", or proximity to a transportation facility or a market or recreational opportunities.

Cost-benefit analysis is any systematic comparison of what a system/program/activity or capital good will cost–usually over its useful life–compared with the revenues or benefits that will be generated. In modern usage, particularly in the Department of Defense and other government agencies, this has meant translating payoffs or benefits into quantitative terms and eventually into such comparisons as dollar costs per lives saved or enemy killed.

DECISION-MAKING CONDITIONS

Decision-making is done under **conditions of certainty, risk** or **uncertainty**. These terms refer to the probability of the outcomes, payoffs, or expected results associated with a given course of action or choice. Probability is the likelihood that something will happen expressed as a value from 0 to 1.0 (which can be thought of as a percentage chance of occurrence–for example, .5 = 50%).

Under **certainty**, the outcome or payoff for an alternative or choice has a probability of 1.0. There are few real world examples–maybe in a choice between types or locations of savings accounts, or whether the banks will actually pay the interest.

Risk is one of the probability conditions under which decisions are made. Under risk the probability of an event or state of nature is known or can be estimated from experience–that is, it can be assigned a value from 0 to 1.0.

Under conditions of **uncertainty** the probability of an event or state of nature (war or peace, prosperity or depression, high interest rates or low) is unknown and cannot be estimated from experience. Strategies followed in this circumstance include minimax (minimize the maximum possible loss), maximin (maximize the minimum payoff), among others.

Some people think that most management decisions are made under conditions of risk, and some people would argue that most of them are made under conditions of uncertainty.

PAYOFF MATRIX

One of the tools that is used in decision-making under conditions of risk is a Payoff Table or Payoff Matrix. Look at Figure 2-1 on the following page.

Across the top of the Payoff Matrix we have three column headings. The first main column is labeled **Strategies** (sometimes called alternatives, options or choices). These are the different things that you can do. Typically you have two or more strategies if you have a choice to make, and this could be between anything. It could be choosing between two persons for a roommate; it could be choosing among buying the cheap machine, the middle-priced machine or the expensive machine; it could be among locating the factory in Alabama, Tennessee or New York.

PAYOFF MATRIX

STRATEGIES OR ALTERNATIVES	STATES OF NATURE			TOTAL EXPECTED VALUE
	ECONOMY POOR (.1)	ECONOMY AVERAGE (.5)	ECONOMY GOOD (.4)	
A. **SMALL MACHINE**	Conditional Value +$500	Conditional Value +$500	Conditional Value +$500	+$500
	Expected Value +$50	Expected Value +$250	Expected Value +$200	
B. **MEDIUM MACHINE**	Conditional Value +$100	Conditional Value +$400	Conditional Value +$800	+$530
	Expected Value +$10	Expected Value +$200	Expected Value +$320	
C. **HUGE MACHINE**	Conditional Value (-$200)	Conditional Value +$300	Conditional Value +$1500	+$730
	Expected Value (-$20)	Expected Value +$150	Expected Value +$600	

FIGURE 2-1

The next column is labeled **States of Nature**. States of Nature represents different things that might happen. This is the environment in which our alternatives are going to be operating. The States of Nature used depend on what you are interested in. If you are a military planner it might be war versus peace, or it might be war with country X, or war with country Y, or war with country Z, or war with all three of them combined.

The final column is labeled **Total Expected Value**.

Under States of Nature in Figure 2-1, we have three economic possibilities: a poor, an average, and a good economy. We can define these in terms of whatever you wish–gross national product, employment, whatever.

For each of those poor, average, and good economic conditions we have a probability. These probabilities can be arrived at by methods ranging from past experience to guess work. In this case, we have said the probability of the economy being poor is one out of ten (.1 or 10%). The probability of it being average is 50-50 (.5). That leaves the chances of things being good at .4, because all of these probabilities have to add up to 1.0 for certainty.

Now, look at our alternatives for each state of nature. We have some measure of payoff, or value, for each alternative. This might be the profit that we are expecting to make from the alternative, or the number of sales we are going to make, or whatever measure we are using for the value of the alternative.

Figure 2-1 shows the conditional value, or the payoffs, of that particular alternative. **Conditional value** is the payoff that you think would happen under the condition of each of the states of nature. In this particular table the conditional value happens to be the same for Alternative A whether conditions are poor, average or good! We are going to get $500, no matter what. Under Alternative B, the conditional value profit is only going to be $100 if things are bad, $400 if things are average, and $800 if things are good. And in Alternative C you will lose $200 if things are bad, you will make $300 if things are average, but if things are good, you will make $1,500.

To determine **expected values** we are going to take the probabilities associated at the top of the chart with each state of nature and multiply that probability times the contingent value just mentioned. For instance, if you expect a poor state of nature, .1 probability for Alternative A, we will multiply that times 500, which gives 1/10 of 500 or 50. For Alternative B under the poor state of nature the expected value is $10, and for Alternative C, -$200 times .1 equals an expected value of -$20. What we have just produced is the **expected value**. That is the conditional value of the alternative times the probability of the state of nature.

Now, do this with all the states of nature that you are looking at. In this case, we are looking at three states of nature. You can have two or you can have ten, but altogether their possibilities can not add up to more than one. We then add the expected values (the conditional value times the probability). One decision criterion that we might want to use as a rule or basis for making a choice is: which of these alternative courses of action gives us the greatest total expected value? Those are the values in the far right hand column that we get by adding the expected values across all three States of Nature. We see, given the alternatives and their conditional values in this chart, that Alternative A totals out to $500 expected value; B to $530; and C to $730.

Alternative C would give you the greatest payoff on the average. You should also notice that if things are bad, it is also going to give you the greatest loss. In fact, if things are bad, while Alternative A is giving you plus $500, Alternative C is giving you minus $200. To summarize, a payoff matrix is a tool for helping planners to clarify their choices under conditions of risk and to see what one alternative involves compared to others.

Figure 2-2 extends the Payoff Matrix concept to a more personal decision–choice of a roommate.

PAYOFF MATRIX

STRATEGIES or CHOICES	STATES OF NATURE (with probabilities)			TOTAL EXPECTED VALUE
	POOR (.2)	FAIR (.3)	GOOD (.5)	
ALICE ALBERT	Conditional Value 6	Conditional Value 6	Conditional Value 6	6
	Expected Value 1.2	Expected Value 1.8	Expected Value 3.0	
BETTY BOB	Conditional Value 2	Conditional Value 4	Conditional Value 10	6.6
	Expected Value .4	Expected Value 1.2	Expected Value 5	

CONDITIONAL VALUES ARE IN TERMS OF ENJOYABILITY ON A SCALE OF
0 = VERY UNPLEASANT TO 10 = FANTASTIC

FIGURE 2-2

PROBABILITY ANALYSIS: PAYOFF MATRIX

Let's summarize the main ideas:

A **payoff matrix** is a tabular display of two or more strategies or choices; the conditional values of each under two or more possible states of nature; the probabilities of these states of nature; the resulting expected values (probability times conditional value); and the total expected value for each strategy or choice (the sum across all states of nature of the expected values for each choice). Comparison is made between total expected values.

States of nature are future environmental conditions which are listed and assigned a **probability** in a payoff matrix. This probability multiplied by the **conditional value** of a choice or alternative results in an **expected value**.

The conditional value of a choice/strategy/alternative is the payoff or benefit expected under the conditions of a specified state of nature.

Expected value is the contingent value of the choice/alternative multiplied by the probability of the relevant state of nature.

The information shown in a payoff matrix can also be shown as a **decision tree** chart as in Figures 2-3A and 2-3B.

DECISION TREE

STRATEGY OR ALTERNATIVE	STATES OF NATURE (ECONOMY)	PROBABILITY	CONDITIONAL VALUE	EXPECTED VALUE	TOTAL EXPECTED VALUE
A	Poor	.1	$500	$50	
	Average	.5	$500	$250	$500
	Good	.4	$500	$200	
B	Poor	.1	$100	$10	
	Average	.5	$400	$200	$530
	Good	.4	$800	$320	
C	Poor	.1	(-$200)	-$20	
	Average	.5	$300	$150	$730
	Good	.4	$1500	$600	

◖ - chance

▣ - decision

FIGURE 2-3A

DECISION TREE

STRATEGY OR ALTERNATIVE	STATES OF NATURE (ECONOMY)	PROBABILITY	CONDITIONAL VALUE	EXPECTED VALUE	TOTAL EXPECTED VALUE
ALICE ALBERT	Poor	.2	6	1.2	
	Fair	.3	6	1.8	6.0
	Good	.5	6	3.0	
BETTY BOB	Poor	.2	2	.4	
	Fair	.3	4	1.2	6.6
	Good	.5	10	5.0	

CONDITIONAL VALUES ARE IN TERMS OF ENJOYABILITY ON A SCALE OF
0 = VERY UNPLEASANT TO 10 = FANTASTIC

- chance

- decision

FIGURE 2-3B

BREAK-EVEN ANALYSIS

Break-even Charts are frequently discussed under controls, but they are certainly useful in planning as well. Here we ask you to refer to the chart, shown as Figure 2-4A.

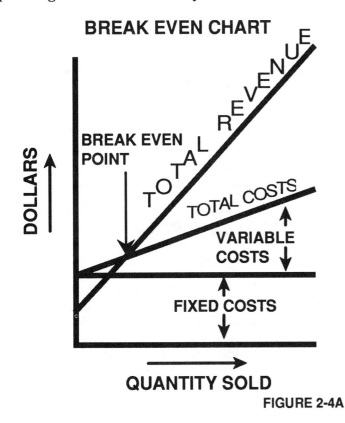

FIGURE 2-4A

25

On the **vertical axis** we have **dollars** going from zero at the bottom to many dollars at the top. And on the **horizontal axis** we have **quantity sold** that starts at zero at the left end and increases in number as you move to the right end.

The general idea of the break-even chart is that for any particular quantity sold we are going to be able to tell five points that are important to us. The first is what are our fixed costs? Second is what are our variable costs? Third, what are our total costs? The fourth is related to the first three, total revenue. Then we will be able to determine the fifth which is whether we are making a profit or suffering a loss.

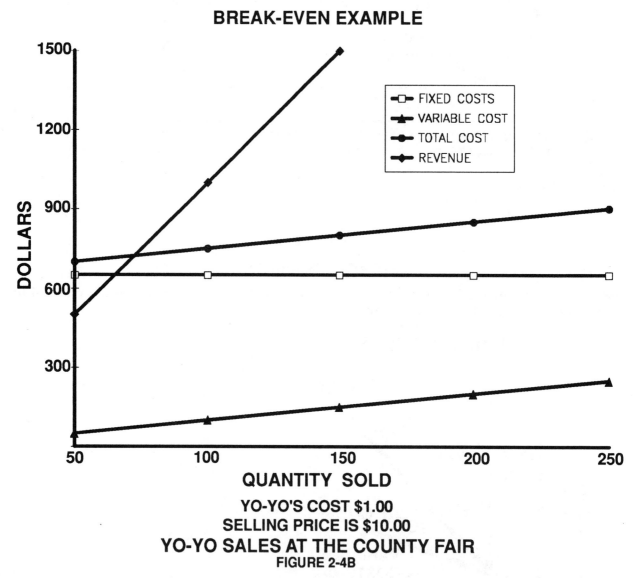

BREAK-EVEN EXAMPLE

YO-YO'S COST $1.00
SELLING PRICE IS $10.00
YO-YO SALES AT THE COUNTY FAIR
FIGURE 2-4B

Let us set up an example using Figure 2-4B. Suppose that you decide to go to the county fair, rent a booth, and sell electronic yo-yos. The county fair lasts three days. It is going to cost $200 a day to rent a booth for a total cost of $600. It is also going to cost $50 for a vendor's license. Everything else will be left out of the equation. You now have **fixed costs** of $650. Even if you do not buy any yo-yos to sell, it is still going to cost you $650. So your losses are $650. Your total costs at that point are only your fixed costs. The fixed costs are those that you have anywhere you are on the line of quantity sold.

Next, let us suppose you bought 250 yo-yos and sold 250 yo-yos. You would be somewhere toward the right end of the line. Your fixed costs for selling 250 yo-yos are still going to be $650; they are fixed, they do not change.

Now, what we are interested in is how many yo-yos you need to sell and how much are you going to have to charge for them in order to cover your fixed costs and variable costs (which is how much, in this case, you pay for the yo-yos)? **Variable costs** are things that vary with the quantity of sales. (We will assume that you can give all the yo-yos you are unable to sell, back to the supplier.)

If you pay $1.00 for each of the yo-yos, and you sell them for $10 each, you can plot out various points on the chart. For instance, we can say if you purchased a hundred yo-yos to sell, your variable costs are $100. Total costs are $100 above fixed costs. At $10 each, 100 sold makes your total revenue $1,000. At that point, revenue is $1,000, fixed cost is $650, and variable cost is $100. $750 is your total cost, leaving you a difference from total revenues of $250–your profit. Your plotted chart would look like Figure 2-4B.

THE ADMINISTRATIVE MAN THEORY OF DECISION-MAKING

Nobel prize winner Herbert Simon, has suggested some real world limits to the use of quantitative models for decision-making. Here are some of the key elements:

> **Economic Man:** in Simon's discussion of decision-making this is the all-knowing, super rational decision-maker of economic theory. He is contrasted with the real world decision-maker–**administrative man.**

> **Administrative Man:** the real world decision-maker of Herbert Simon's creation who is subject to **bounded rationality**, limited psychological problem-processing ability, and restricted knowledge of possible alternatives, their outcomes and their probabilities–all in contrast to the **rational-economic man** of traditional economic theory. Administrative man **satisfices**–accepts the solution that meets his criteria rather than looks for the best possible solution.

> **Optimizing**: the strategy of Simon's mythical rational-economic man who knows all.

> **Bounded rationality**: Herbert Simon's idea that a real-world decision-maker (administrative man) has his thinking limited by such things as societal and organizational norms and the impracticality of obtaining or processing all possible or even nice-to-know information about the problem or alternatives. The result is the use of **Heuristics**, rules of thumb, and **satisficing.**

> **Satisficing** is the decision strategy followed by Simon's real-world **administrative man** in contrast to **economic man's** optimizing. Satisficing is choosing the first alternative that meets the criteria rather than looking for the best possible choice.

NAMES TO REMEMBER:

Peter Drucker - Eight Key Results Areas; Management by Objectives

Herbert Simon - administrative man model of decision-making; 3 phases of decision making (Nobel prize winner)

KEY WORDS, PHRASES, AND ABBREVIATIONS:

(write out definitions and examples below)

Administrative Man

alternative

alternative course of action

bounded rationality

brainstorming

break-even chart/table

break-even point

budget

certainty

choice phase

conditional value

contingency planning/plans

cost-benefit analysis

decision-making

decision tree

Delphi Method

design phase

economic forecasting

Economic Man

expected value

expert opinion

fixed costs

forecasting

goals

hierarchy of plans

innovation

intelligence phase

Key Result Areas (Drucker)

long-range plans/planning

Management by Objectives/MBO

mission/mission statement

manager performance and development

market research

market share

objectives

operational planning

optimizing

payoff matrix/table

planning

planning process

policy

premises of planning

primacy of planning

procedure

probability

productivity

problem-solving

profitability

program

project

rational economic man

resources

responsibility

risk

rolling plan

rule

sales forecasting

satisficing

short-range plans/planning

single-use plans

social responsibilities

social and political forecasting

standing plans

states of nature

statistical methods in forecasting

strategy

technological forecasting

total costs (break-even)

total revenues (break-even)

uncertainty

variable costs (break-even)

worker performance and morale

WOTS-UP analysis

Chapter 2: Sample Questions

1. Which of the following would NOT be part of the planning process:

   (A) forecasting
   (B) problem and opportunity analysis
   (C) developing alternatives
   (D) putting people into the organizational structure
   (E) decision-making

2. Detailed technical and operational planning for the immediate future would be associated with:

   (A) top management
   (B) middle management
   (C) first-line management
   (D) Board of Directors
   (E) stockholders

3. Strategic planning is the responsibility primarily of:

   (A) top management
   (B) middle management
   (C) first-line management
   (D) supervisors
   (E) union organizers

4. The term "hierarchy of plans" means that:

   (A) operational plans are developed from controls
   (B) planning proceeds from mission to objectives to strategies to operational plans
   (C) in large organizations standing plans dictate day-to-day strategy
   (D) both A and B but not C
   (E) none of the above

5. A statement of required or prohibited behavior (action) is called a:

   (A) rule
   (B) responsibility
   (C) reference point
   (D) result area
   (E) time-frame

6. Policies (1) _____ whereas, rules (2) _____ .

   (A) (1) specify behavior, (2) guide action
   (B) (1) are made by top management, (2) are made by middle management
   (C) (1) are standing plans, (2) are single-use plans
   (D) (1) guide decisions, (2) require or prohibit specific actions
   (E) none of the above

7. Which of the following is NOT a type of standing plan?

    (A) policy
    (B) procedure
    (C) rule
    (D) budget
    (E) both C and D but not A and B

8. Market share, innovation, productivity are three of the eight "Key Results Areas" of:

    (A) Peter the Great
    (B) "Peter and the Wolf"
    (C) Peter Drucker
    (D) Peter, Paul, and Mary
    (E) Herbert Simon

9. A budget is (or may be) a plan:

    (A) for use of resources
    (B) for expected results
    (C) stated in numbers (often monetary units)
    (D) used as a control tool
    (E) all of the above

10. The checklist which aircraft pilots go through prior to takeoff is one form of:

    (A) budget
    (B) policy
    (C) procedure
    (D) rule
    (E) strategy

11. Decision-making involves:

    (A) action
    (B) controlling
    (C) choosing among alternatives
    (D) managers rather than staff persons
    (E) the final step in the planning process

12. In a break-even chart the horizontal axis shows:

    (A) dollars
    (B) quantity sold
    (C) per capita income
    (D) total revenues
    (E) net income

Chapter 2: Answers

1. D   A, B, C, and E are all part of planning. D is part of the staffing function.

2. C   First-line management would be the best answer.

3. A   Top management is clearly the management level most responsible for strategic (long-range) planning.

4. B   B describes the hierarchy of plans.

5. A   Rule—dictates behavior.

6. D   Policies are guides to thought whereas rules dictate/prescribe action.

7. D   A budget is one kind of "single-use" plan. Most budgets are for a specified period of time.

8. C   Peter Drucker

9. E   All of the above.

10. C   Procedure—a standing plan which specifies a series of steps.

11. C   Choice among alternative solutions or courses of action is the essence of decision-making.

12. B   Quantity sold is usually shown on the horizontal axis of a break-even chart.

Chapter 3: Organizing

Organizing is the management function that divides the work that will need to be done; groups tasks into positions, work groups, and departments; and establishes a structure of authority relationships and ways of coordinating activities.

The **organizing process** determines what tasks will have to be done to accomplish objectives; how those tasks will be grouped together into positions and those in turn into departments; and how positions and departments relate to one another.

An **organization** is a social system whose components are coordinated in pursuit of a common mission or unifying goals and whose members share perceptions of the organization's boundaries.

An **organization chart** is a diagram showing authority relationships between positions and departments in an organization.

AUTHORITY AND HIERARCHY

Authority: line authority is the right to act, to decide, to command. **Staff authority** is the right to give advice and recommendations to those in line positions.

Responsibility is an obligation or assignment to achieve some goal or result. In classical theory, it should be accompanied by enough authority to do the job.

Accountability is the obligation to report on the use and results of an assignment of authority (similar to responsibility).

A **reporting relationship** is the relationship of subordinate to superior in an authority hierarchy. The subordinate is responsible to the superior for his/her actions and results and must report on or account for them.

The **chain of command** is the line of direct superior-subordinate authority relationships running from top to bottom of the hierarchy.

LINE AND STAFF

The terms line and staff refer to both positions and authority relations. **Line positions** are those which contribute directly to the main purpose or mission of the organization—e.g., combat arms as opposed to the Judge Advocate General in the Army, or the sales people as opposed to the president of the company in a marketing organization. In a manufacturing company, line positions are usually defined as including production, marketing, and finance in contrast to staff positions that provide support, advice, and assistance to the line positions.

Line authority is the right to decide, act, and command those directly subordinate to the line position. A sales manager, for example, has line authority over all people in his sales department; a company commander has line authority over all soldiers in the company.

Staff positions are those which support and give advice to line positions, for example, in a manufacturing firm, the legal staff or the medical staff.

Staff authority involves a relationship in which the staff position provides advice and recommendations to a line position but cannot act or command action in areas of the line position's authority or jurisdiction.

Functional authority is a variant of staff authority in which staff managers may give narrow technical advice or direction to subordinates of line managers within a carefully limited scope.

For example, the Controller may issue instructions to the bookkeeping staff in a production operation under the supervision of the vice president of manufacturing on how certain reports are to be prepared.

Classical management theory or classical management principles, narrowly defined, are the views associated with Henri Fayol about how organizations ought to be managed. They usually take a top-down view and analyze and describe the organization as though it were a closed system—independent from other organizations and influences.

Fayol proposed the five functions of management: planning, organizing (including staffing), commanding, coordinating and controlling.

Fayol also outlined 14 principles of management which many of his followers believe apply to all organizations. These include statements about division of work, authority and responsibility, unity of command, unity of direction, and *esprit de corps.*

Principles of organization is a term usually associated with classical management and would include Fayol's 14 principles—among them unity of command, unity of direction, authority equal to responsibility, etc.

SOME CLASSICAL OR TRADITIONAL PRINCIPLES OF MANAGEMENT

Unity of direction is a classical principle of management stated by Fayol. It says that all activities in pursuit of a given organizational goal should be under the direction of a single person.

Unity of command also is one of Fayol's 14 classical principles of management. It says that each subordinate should have only one boss.

Scalar principle is another of Fayol's 14 classical principles. It states that there should be a single, clear, and unbroken line of authority from the top of the organization to each subordinate position (also called the **chain of command principle**).

The exception principle—once procedures, policies, and other plans have been established and are working, management should focus on those cases (exceptions) where performance does not meet standards. This was originally a principle from Scientific Management. It is an important concept for the controlling function.

Specialization is dividing the work into very simple or basic tasks—also called **division of labor.** This makes jobs easy to learn and workers easy to hire, train and replace. Classical and Scientific Management writers believed specialization was needed for efficiency. Most assembly line jobs are highly specialized.

Span of control—there is a limit to the number of subordinates a single person can supervise.

BUREAUCRACY

In the view of many, the application of classical or traditional principles results in an organizational form called **bureaucratic** or **mechanistic**.

Bureaucracy is a form of organization, described in its ideal form by Max Weber as operating in an impersonal way on the basis of written rules and records. It is based on rational-legal authority. The term **mechanistic** refers to an organizational form essentially identical to bureaucracy—centralized, hierarchical, guided by rules and written procedures, with highly specialized jobs. Typically it is rigid and inflexible but tends to work well in a stable, predictable environment and technology. This is in contrast to **organic** organizational forms. Organic organizations are more informal, less hierarchically structured, and have less rigid specialization with a greater degree of personal relationships; supposedly, they are more flexible and responsive to changing environments and technologies.

OTHER NON-TRADITIONAL VIEWS

In contrast to the classical, traditional, and bureaucratic view that authority is ordained by law and position, is Chester Barnard's **Acceptance Theory of Authority.** In this view, authority depends for its effectiveness on whether or not it is accepted by those to whom communications or commands are given. Authority is like a hunting license; it does not guarantee compliance but requires some leadership skills to make it work.

System 4 Organization is a participative or collegial form of organization proposed by Rensis Likert. It is based on:

1) the principle of supportive relationships,

2) overlapping group form of management, and

3) high performance standards.

An overlapping group structure was advocated by Rensis Likert as a characteristic of his System 4 form of management. The organization is managed as a collection of interlocking groups. Relations are between a superior manager/leader and his/her group or team rather than the one-to-one relations of traditional organization.

Linking pin—in Likert's System 4 overlapping group organizational structure, the groups are tied together by people with membership in two or more groups, often as subordinate member of a higher group and leader of the next lower level group—as a vice president of marketing is part of the CEO's **team** and head of another group in marketing. Such people are called linking pins.

DEPARTMENTATION

Departmentation is the grouping together of positions, their functions and responsibilities, under parts or departments of the organization structure.

Bases of departmentation—is the logic or rationale underlying the grouping of activities in an organization. **Internal bases** include functional (by specialty), product and process; **external bases** include geography and customer.

TYPES OF DEPARTMENTATION

Functional departmentation is the most common form of departmentation. It groups positions together on the basis of common professional activities, or common organization-wide purpose or function. Examples are engineering, production, finance, marketing, and personnel. The benefits of functional organization are that specialists work together and duplication and overlap are reduced. Drawbacks tend to be a loss of sight of organization-wide objectives and difficulty in getting support and cooperation for new products and programs.

Process departmentation is done on the basis of different technologies or steps in a process—e.g., receiving, shipping, stamping, welding, painting, and assembly.

Product departmentation puts together all of the positions and activities in support of different products or product types in separate and often independent departments or divisions. An example would be a company with divisions of **bulk chemicals, cosmetics,** and **food products,** each of which has functional departments of production, marketing, finance, etc.

Customer departmentation is organization on the basis of customers, or types of customers, found particularly in marketing organizations. Examples would be departments and managers for national accounts, military sales, automobile manufacturers, etc.

Geographical or territorial departmentation (common in sales and military organizations) is based on a division of the service area on lines of accessibility, similarity of clients and problems, etc. Examples: CINCPAC, CINCLANT; or West Coast Sales Division; Central Division; Eastern Division; Southern Division; Latin American Division.

Mixed departmentation as the name implies, describes an organization that uses two or more different bases of departmentation, usually at different levels—e.g., functional at the first level and regional at the next level down.

Project organization/departmentation brings together people, positions, or work groups in support of a specific objective or task—usually of a limited nature and only for the time required or allowed to complete the project. For example, putting together a display of the company's manufacturing skills and products at a world trade fair might require a project team from marketing, engineering, production, and perhaps others.

Matrix organization is an innovative development in which (typically) a project or product form of organization is superimposed on top of a functional organization. The forerunner of the matrix form was the task force—similar to the project form of departmentation. A matrix structure is intended to provide flexibility along with improved coordination and cooperation between people from different functional departments in support of a special product or program. For example, the F-22 program manager under a matrix organization might have assigned to him semi-permanently people from engineering, research and development, finance, marketing, production and so forth.

STRATEGY AND STRUCTURE

A business historian, A.D. Chandler has hypothesized that organizations that changed from a single-business strategy to diversification (many different products or businesses) also changed in organizational structure from a centralized functional-departmentation form to a decentralized product-department form (also called a multi-division form). This is called the strategy-structure hypothesis.

SPAN OF CONTROL AND ORGANIZATIONAL SHAPE

Span of control is the number of persons supervised by a given manager (also, the number of other positions supervised by any one position). In general, how wide the span of control is or should be depends on the actual persons involved as well as the nature of the work. **Narrow spans of control** (few supervised) are associated with tall organizational structures; under **broad spans** (when many are supervised) the organization structure tends to be flat.

Tall structure is an organization with many levels of supervision or hierarchy and (usually) small (narrow) spans of control.

A **flat** organizational structure is found in an organization with very few levels of hierarchy. A wide span of control is usually associated with a flat structure (as, also, may be delegation and decentralization).

CENTRALIZATION, DECENTRALIZATION, DELEGATION

Centralization involves an organizational structure and associated policies and procedures that puts the making of the most important decisions, as well as authority and responsibility, at the center (usually meaning the top) of the organization, corporate headquarters. One of Fayol's 14 principles favors centralization, as a rule.

Decentralization involves moving decision making, authority, and responsibility to lower levels of the organization and/or out from corporate headquarters and into the field.

Delegation is the assignment of responsibility and the necessary authority to a subordinate. At the same time, overall or final responsibility cannot be delegated and remains with the superior.

FACTORS AFFECTING STRUCTURE

The environment of organizations includes the legal system, technology, the economy, other organizations, the physical world, and a variety of stakeholders. Environments have been characterized in terms of stability, complexity, and certainty.

In general, more stable environments favor mechanistic forms of organization, whereas organic forms of organization work better when the environment is rapidly changing and hard to predict.

Mechanistic organizations have a higher degree of formalization than do organic ones. **Formalization** is the extent to which an organization depends on written rules, procedures and similar documents.

Other factors affecting organization design include complexity and interdependence. **Complexity** is the number of different kinds of jobs together with the number of levels of hierarchy in the organization. In general, the greater the **interdependence** between the various parts of an organization, the greater will be the need for coordinating mechanisms.

Technology—both its type and how fast it is changing—in the contingency views of organization design are among the determinants of the effectiveness of any particular form of organization. Three types of technology distinguished by Joan Woodward are:

1) **Unit and small batch** refer to a one-of-a-kind (tailor-made) or job-shop form of production found in such diverse businesses as men's tailors, yacht and airplane manufacture.

2) **Mass production/assembly line technology** is related to variations in organizational structure. Mechanistic structures seem to work best with this type of technology.

3) **Continuous process technology (CPT)** is seen in oil refineries, soap factories, and some food production. The plant is a big machine with the raw materials being fed into one end and the finished product coming out the other.

JOB ORGANIZATION AND DESIGN

The specialization and standardization of work were carried to their extreme in the moving assembly line introduced by Henry Ford. A job which consisted of tightening a few nuts thousands of times a day was demoralizing. Because the worker was easily replaceable, he was usually insecure and often turned to unions to find job security.

In the 1960's Herzberg's motivator-hygiene theory of motivation led to attempts to restore work motivation through **job enrichment**. This consisted of redesigning jobs so they held more **motivator factors**—responsibility, opportunities for professional growth, achievement, and recognition.

Job enrichment, whatever the approach, implies increasing the depth of the job, adding to it **vertically** by giving the job planning and controlling elements.

In contrast, **job enlargement** increases the scope of the job **horizontally** by adding duties of a similar level of skill at the same organizational level. Herzberg calls this **horizontal loading**—"washing dishes, washing silver, washing pans—it's still the same job."

NAMES TO REMEMBER:

Chester Barnard   -   the acceptance theory of authority

Henri Fayol   -   Father of modern management, classical approach, first stated the functions of management, fourteen classical principles of management

Rensis Likert   -   System 4 management, linking pins, overlapping group mode of management

Frederick Taylor   -   Father of Scientific Management

Max Weber   -   bureaucracy

Joan Woodward   -   technology types

KEY WORDS, PHRASES, AND ABBREVIATIONS:

(write out definitions or examples below)

acceptance theory of authority

accountability

authority

bases of departmentation

bureaucracy

chain of command

classical management theory/principles

continuous process technology

customer departmentation

centralization

decentralization

delegation

departmentation

environment

exception principle

flat (structure)

functional authority

functional departmentation

geographical/territorial departmentation

hierarchy

hierarchical structure

job enlargement

job enrichment

line, line authority

linking pin

mass production/assembly line technology

matrix organization

organic

organization

organization chart

organizing function

overlapping group structure

principles of organization

product departmentation

project organization/departmentation

reporting relationship

responsibility

scalar principle

span of control

specialization

staff

staff authority

System 4 Organization

tall structure

technology

unit and small batch

unity of command

unity of direction

Chapter 3: Sample Questions

1. The XYZ Corporation has Division Sales Directors for Eastern, Midwestern, and Western Districts. Under each is a Manager for Farm Products, for Industrial Goods, for Restaurant Supplies, and for Retail Consumer Products. The basis of departmentation at the district level is (1)_____ and at the lower level (2)_____.

   (A) (1) legal, (2) functional
   (B) (1) functional, (2) geographical
   (C) (1) regular, (2) ad hoc
   (D) (1) geographical or territorial, (2) product or customer
   (E) none of the above

2. Atlas Aircraft Industries (AAI) has created the Zeppelin Program headed by Frank Smith as program manager. Assigned to Smith for the duration of the program are an accountant from the Controller's office, a financial analyst from the Vice President (VP) for Finance, two design engineers who work for VP of Engineering, two whiz kids from Research and Development, a production man from VP of Production, two people from VP of Marketing, and a training specialist from VP of Personnel. The type of organization structure in use here seems to be:

   (A) simple form
   (B) functional
   (C) fractional
   (D) matrix
   (E) product

3. Woodward found that the classical and bureaucratic guidelines seemed to work best in connection with which type of technology?

   (A) unit and small batch
   (B) manual labor
   (C) computerized
   (D) high tech
   (E) none of the above

4. In the Thrombosis Supply Company, the Controller is authorized to give directions on accounting procedures to the bookkeepers at each of the regional sales offices. What kind of authority is involved here?

   (A) line
   (B) professional
   (C) functional
   (D) informal
   (E) none of the above

5. The right to act and to command is associated with:

   (A) automatic authority
   (B) functional authority
   (C) line authority
   (D) staff authority
   (E) virtual authority

6. The right or obligation to give advice and make recommendations but without the right to act or command defines:

   (A) altruistic authority
   (B) line authority
   (C) staff authority
   (D) command authority
   (E) universal authority

7. Classical principles of organization state that:

   (A) final responsibility cannot be delegated
   (B) responsibility should equal authority
   (C) authority should equal responsibility
   (D) each subordinate should report to only one boss
   (E) all of the above

8. According to the organizing principle of _____, all activities directed toward the same goal should be under the direction of one person.

   (A) unity of authority
   (B) unified goals
   (C) unity of command
   (D) unity of direction
   (E) none of the above

9. The Bravo Brothers factory is organized into five sections: 1) Receiving and Warehouse; 2) Stamping; 3) Assembly; 4) Finishing; and 5) Shipping. The factory is organized on which basis or principle:

   (A) customer
   (B) functional
   (C) departmental
   (D) process
   (E) product

10. Under the functional structure:

    (A) specialists have the benefit of working together
    (B) departments tend to lose sight of organization-wide objectives
    (C) it is often difficult to get support needed for new products
    (D) duplication of scarce resources is reduced
    (E) all of the above

11. In the area of the organization of individual jobs or job design, one approach emphasizes increasing the scope or range of the job so that the number of activities of the worker is increased. This approach is called:

    (A) job enlargement
    (B) job enrichment
    (C) job entitlement
    (D) job posting
    (E) job specialization

12. A characteristic of the design of work in Henry Ford's moving assembly line was:

    (A) highly specialized jobs
    (B) a preponderance of craft-like, diversified jobs
    (C) what today would be called "job enrichment"
    (D) extremely low wages compared to other employers
    (E) none of the above

13. Disadvantages experienced by organizations with extremely high degrees of job specialization include:

    (A) reduced motivation
    (B) high turnover (quitting)
    (C) high absenteeism
    (D) all of the above
    (E) none of the above

14. Advantages of the functional basis for departmentation include all of the following EXCEPT:

    (A) efficient use of resources
    (B) simplified training of functional specialists
    (C) improved coordination between different functional departments
    (D) preserves strategic control at top of the organization
    (E) None of the above are exceptions. All are advantages of functional departmentation.

15. Advantages of departmentation on the basis of products include which of the following?

    (A) make growth easier
    (B) make coordination between functions easier
    (C) focus on client wants rather than interests internal to firm
    (D) all of the above
    (E) none of the above

16. According to Burns and Stalker, compared to "organic" systems, "mechanistic" systems seem to be more appropriate and effective for:

    (A) stable technologies and markets
    (B) rapidly changing technologies
    (C) rapidly changing markets
    (D) organizations where coordination is by mutual adjustment
    (E) none of the above

1. D   The division-level organization is geographical or territorial while at the next level down, the basis of organization is by product or customer. "Restaurant Supplies" could be a grouping of specialized product or a grouping in terms of a distribution channel—restaurant supply houses or restaurants.

2. D   This is a matrix form of organization with a program, project, or task force organization of a semi-permanent nature overlaid on a functional structure.

3. E   Woodward found that the classical, bureaucratic (also called mechanistic) organization form worked best with mass-production/assembly line technology—so the answer is none of the above.

4. C   This is an example of functional authority. The sales managers would have line authority over those bookkeepers assigned to them.

5. C   Line authority—the right to command all direct subordinates.

6. C   Staff authority is limited to giving advice and making recommendations. The same person may have line authority in relation to his/her subordinates and staff authority with respect to a superior.

7. E   All are classical principles of organization. A, B, and C deal with the equality of authority and responsibility. D is the principle of unity of command.

8. D   Unity of direction urges that all efforts toward the same goal be under a single direction.

9. D   The Bravo factory is organized on the basis of different processes, different steps in the overall production process.

10. E   All of the above are true. A and D are advantages of a functional structure; B and C are disadvantages.

11. A   Job enlargement

12. A   Highly specialized jobs

13. D   All of the above. Certainly true of production jobs. May not be true for professions.

14. C   Coordination between departments is more difficult. Therefore, C is not one of the advantages.

15. D   All of the above. Coordination between functions is easier because the functional managers report to a product manager.

16. A   Stable technologies and markets—typical of mass production (assembly line) industries.

Chapter 4: Staffing

The **staffing function** is one of the basic management functions of planning, organizing, etc. It provides the right people to fill the structure designed by the organizing function.

Human resources management and **personnel management** are names used synonymously for the administration of the staffing function.

The **staffing process** is the same as the personnel process (or human resources process). It includes manpower planning, recruitment, selection, orientation, training and development, compensation, promotion and job assignment, performance appraisal, health and safety, and retirement.

An important question in human resource planning is whether to adopt a policy of **promotion** (and selection for vacant positions in general) **from within** the organization—that is from among those already employed by it—or to seek the best candidates, from whatever source, whether from outside or within the organization. In general, promotion-from-within policies seem to have positive benefits for employee morale but often at the cost of severely restricting sources of competent replacements.

Manpower planning is the application of the planning function to the personnel area, that is, to the staffing function. The term has overtones of large-scale and grandiose plans such as a government, army or other very large organization might undertake. Basically, it involves figuring out the kind, skills and number of people needed in the future, and how to insure that they will be available.

An employee inventory chart is a written record, list, or display showing present employees and such information as their ages, qualifications and potential for promotion, possible successors, present level of performance, and similar information that might aid in personnel planning. Obviously a rather confidential document, it is a useful planning tool. Such records go by a variety of names such as **skills inventory, replacement charts, manpower audit**, and **personal data sheet**.

JOB ANALYSIS

A central activity in staffing is **job analysis**—the collection and study of information about a job or jobs that leads to job descriptions and job specifications and is a prerequisite to job evaluation.

A **job** is a group of positions that have very similar duties, tasks and activities—for example, secretary, sales manager, or electrician.

A **job description** lists the various tasks comprising a job, the function or purpose of the job, and its relation to other jobs.

A **job specification** is a description of the qualifications required by a person to perform a particular job. This would include education and training, skill level, physical or health attributes, etc.

THE LEGAL ENVIRONMENT

The staffing function is subject to a variety of Federal, state and local laws and regulations. Two areas of great interest in recent years are Equal Employment Opportunity (EEO) and Safety and Health.

Equal Employment Opportunity (EEO)—refers to legislation and governmental and organizational policies that require that all persons have the same treatment in employment decisions regardless of race, national origin, age, religion or sex.

Some EEO legislation includes:

Equal Pay Act of 1963—provides that men and women performing the same work must get the same pay.

Civil Rights Act of 1964—a major piece of the structure of civil rights and equal employment opportunity (EEO) legislation in the U.S. Title VII forbids discrimination in employment based on race, religion, national origin, or sex.

Title VII—refers to the section of the Civil Rights Act of 1964 (as amended) which outlaws discrimination in employment (hiring, promotions, job assignments, etc.) on basis of race, color, religion, national origin, or sex.

The Equal Employment Opportunity Commission (EEOC)—established by the federal government (and various other jurisdictions) to administer equal employment opportunity legislation.

Uniform Guidelines—a set of rules and interpretations of legislation and judicial decisions in the area of equal employment opportunity, published in 1978 by the federal Equal Employment Opportunity Commission, the Department of Justice, the Labor Department, and the Civil Service Commission. The uniform guidelines provide that all procedures (tests, performance appraisals, etc.) used as a basis for staffing decisions be demonstrably valid and relevant to job performance. The full title is **Uniform Guidelines on Employee Selection Procedures**.

OSHA (Occupational Safety and Health Act) covers a different area from that of EEO laws, but is, like them, part of the environment of legislation and governmental regulation that affects the staffing function.

OSHA—Occupational Safety and Health Act (1970)—establishes standards for health and safety at work and provides for their administration (and further elaboration) by an **Occupational Safety and Health Administration** (also called OSHA). This is an example of an externally imposed control. Internal organizational responsibility for implementation is frequently found in the production department. Some organizations have a separate department concerned with safety and health which is sometimes part of the personnel department.

RECRUITMENT AND SELECTION

Recruitment is the part of the personnel or staffing process that involves attracting job candidates to the organization so that they may go through the selection process.

Selection process is the part of the staffing function and personnel process concerned with gathering information about job candidates and choosing those who meet the organization's criteria.

Application blank is any form on which the employer asks the candidate to provide information for hiring decisions. Completion of an application is usually an early step in the recruiting/hiring process and is governed by EEO legislation and the 1978 Uniform Guidelines.

Bona Fide Occupational Qualifications (BFOQ) requires that a job candidate's race, color, age, sex, or national origin may not be considered or asked about in the hiring process unless legitimately related to the job (as would be the religion of candidates for the job of pastor of a church).

Employment test is any instrument for sampling the performance of a candidate to get information to be used in making a decision about employment. Types of employment tests include pencil and paper tests of verbal or quantitative skills or clerical ability, as well as simulations or actual work performance.

Reference refers to a person said by the job candidate to know about some (or all) of the employee's qualifications for employment (e.g., experience, knowledge, education, personal traits, etc.). A widely held principle of selection is that references should always be checked.

An **employment interview** is any conversation between a candidate and one or more employer interviewers that is intended to help in deciding about hiring. The **final interview** is between the candidate and the prospective supervisor or person who makes the final hiring decision, as opposed to a **screening interview** or preliminary interviews.

> **Non-directive interviews** allow the interview candidate considerable freedom in the content, sequence, and detail of what is discussed. The interviewer guides the interview by use of **open-ended questions** (like "Tell me about yourself," or "What was that job like?") and **probes** (such as "I see," "I'm not sure I understand," "Tell me more," "Why?").
>
> **Directive interviews** tend to use more closed or focused questions (such as, "What were your responsibilities in that job?" "How large was your territory?").
>
> **Structured interviews** require all interviewers to ask essentially the same questions in the same sequence. This tends to increase the degree of agreement between interviewers (inter-interviewer reliability).
>
> **Unstructured interviews** leave the choice of questions and the order in which they are asked up to the individual interviewers.

Interviewer bias or errors in judgment—common sources of error or interviewer bias include:

> **Halo effect**—allowing one trait such as physical appearance to influence judgments about other, not necessarily related, traits such as honesty.
>
> **Stereotyping**—judging an individual on the basis of membership in some group whose alleged characteristics the individual may or may not share.

Physical examination—in some organizations and occupations it is a regular part of the employment/hiring process, usually the last step.

Assessment Center is a method for selecting among job or training candidates. It uses a variety of measures of aptitudes, skill, and knowledge including leaderless group discussions, paper-and-pencil tests, and oral presentations. Panels of trained and experienced observers rate the performance of the candidates. Research reports on the validity and reliability of this selection method are generally favorable.

TRAINING AND HUMAN RESOURCE DEVELOPMENT

Human resource development includes training, education, various forms of job rotation and planned career experiences intended to enhance the employee's ability, performance and value to the organization.

Training is the subfield of personnel/human resources management concerned with developing employees and helping them acquire the knowledge, skills and attitudes needed to achieve organizational goals.

Development is another name for training. It is usually used when referring to training for managers and executives.

Orientation is the process by which new employees are introduced and told about the organization's rules, benefits, pay arrangements, insurance and so forth. Orientation is often treated as being distinct from training.

TYPES OF TRAINING

An important first step in planning any training or development program would be a **needs assessment** to determine training goals which in turn affect methods used.

OJT (on-the-job-training) may be the oldest form of employee training, one still widely used today. The essence of OJT is that the employee is productively employed—actually turning out a product or performing a service—at the same time he is learning the job.

Vestibule training differs from OJT in that the training is done in a separate area (a vestibule) that is part of the factory or work area but not actually on the production line or part of the main flow of work. The output may still contribute to the total production of goods or services but the training process is sheltered somewhat from the pressures of a regular work station.

Apprenticeship is a form of training, used mostly in skilled trades and involving lengthy study and work experiences under skilled workers (journeymen).

Job rotation is a technique of training and development used especially for managerial or professional employees. This technique is often used with hourly or non-supervisory employees as a method for **enriching** the job (or at least relieving boredom) by moving the employee around among duties.

COMPENSATION AND BENEFITS

Wage and salary administration is the same thing as compensation management.

Compensation management is the specialized field within human resources management/personnel that is concerned with using pay and benefits most effectively to achieve the goals of the staffing functions. At a minimum it includes job evaluation—the process of determining the wages to be paid for various jobs. More broadly, it aims at enhancing employee work motivation.

Job evaluation is the process of assigning a monetary value to a job.

Compensation is any good or service given to an employee in exchange for his/her services. Compensation includes not only monetary payment, but also other benefits like insurance, housing, vacations and the like.

Benefits are whatever goods or services an organization gives an employee in exchange for work. **Benefits** usually refer to compensation other than money—such as insurance, company car, education costs, etc.

Performance appraisal is the measurement or description of job performance by an employee, usually done by the employee's supervisor, and usually with feedback to the employee through an interview or a copy of the appraisal. This is a technique of control.

Disciplinary action usually means some form of punishment administered by management. Punishment can range from oral warnings and written reprimands, to layoff and firing.

Retirement is often viewed as the terminal stage in the staffing or personnel process—from the employee's point of view it is the end of his/her active career with the organization. Retirement programs and planning are usually a responsibility of the personnel department.

ERISA (Employee Retirement Income Security Act of 1974) establishes standards for company retirement plans.

LABOR RELATIONS AND UNIONS

Labor relations—also called **industrial relations**—is the aspect of personnel or human resources management that deals with organized labor. The field of academic study of unions, labor legislation, collective bargaining, etc.

A **Union** is a group of employees who form an association for the purpose of improving the conditions of their employment.

THE STRUCTURE OF ORGANIZED LABOR IN THE U.S.

AFL-CIO (The American Federation of Labor–Congress of Industrial Organizations) is a confederation or umbrella organization of almost 100 independent national unions representing about four-fifths of unionized workers in the U.S.

National union formulates policy, represents and lobbies for the union members and subordinate levels of organization at the national and state level. They may conduct nation-wide or even international industry-wide contract negotiations. An example is the United Auto Workers (UAW).

Local (union)—in the structure of the labor movement in the U.S., the self-governing unit closest to the actual worker is called a local. In an industrial union it will usually include all of the employees of a specific plant; in a teacher's union, the teachers of a particular school district; in a craft union, the workers of a defined geographic area (e.g., a county). In some industries locals bargain independently for contracts; in others there are industry wide negotiations plus local negotiations.

TYPES OF UNIONS

Craft (union)—is made up of workers in the same skill or craft such as plumbers, carpenters, bricklayers, and the like. The construction industry is dominated by craft unions.

General (union)—one that seeks or accepts members from any occupation, industry, or line of work. The teamsters' union is a prominent example.

Association—as used in names of labor organizations, such as National Education Association or Policemen's Benevolent Association, is simply a euphemism for **union.**

Industrial union—one that limits its membership to employees of a particular industry—such as automobiles or steel—or to a particular organization (Ford), or factory. The essence of the industrial union is that all employees of the unionized company, regardless of their specific work, are members of the same industrial union—pipe fitters, electricians, machinists, welders in an auto plant would all belong to the UAW (United Auto Workers).

U.S. LABOR LEGISLATION AND POLICY

Wagner Act—The National Labor Relations Act of 1935 (NLRA)—the nation's basic labor legislation. See NLRA and NLRB.

NLRA—National Labor Relations Act (1935—The Wagner Act)—the basic labor law in the U.S. It establishes employee rights to form unions, requires employers to bargain with such unions in good faith, and prohibits **unfair labor practices** such as firing employees who join unions.

NLRB—National Labor Relations Board—established originally under The Wagner Act to administer its provisions, supervise representation elections, hear and act on complaints of unfair labor practices, and the like.

Taft-Hartley Act (1947)—tried to balance power more equally between labor and management. Outlawed the closed-shop (which required union membership before employment).

Landrum-Griffin Act (1959)—attempted to eliminate racketeering from organized labor, to promote union democracy and self-government, and to provide for closer supervision by the Federal government.

Organizing process (union)—in labor relations the process regulated and protected by the Wagner Act (NLRA) by which employees organize themselves (or are organized by an existing union) into a union.

Certification—an action by the National Labor Relations Board to officially designate a union as the representative of the employees in a bargaining unit if the union has won a representation election by getting the votes of fifty percent plus one vote of those actually voting. (**Decertification** is the opposite of certification and results from employees voting the union out.)

Collective bargaining is a joint discussion by union and management that attempts to reach agreement on conditions of employment. Federal law (beginning with the Wagner Act) requires employers to engage in good faith collective bargaining with a union certified by the NLRB as the representative of the bargaining unit. Thus, Federal policy is to look at collective bargaining as the basic mechanism for resolving labor disputes. If collective bargaining leads to agreement, the result is a **contract**.

Mediation—any effort of a third party to facilitate resolution of a dispute. Federal and state governments maintain mediation services to help resolve labor disputes and promote collective bargaining agreement. The mediator's job is to help the two parties reach an agreement (as opposed to an arbitrator who decides how the dispute should be resolved.)

Mediator—a third party who tries to help resolve a dispute.

Contract—in the field of labor relations this is the agreement between labor and management that describes conditions of work, rights and obligations of the parties, grievance procedures, etc. to be observed during the period covered.

Contract administration—actions of union and management to carry out and live with the provisions of the contract. The most prominent activity is often the processing of grievances.

Grievance—under most union contracts a grievance is defined as a claim that some specific provision of the contract has been violated.

Grievance procedure—the series of actions or process specified in the contract (of a unionized organization) for dealing with grievances. The first step is usually a request for resolution by the immediate supervisor and the final step is usually compulsory arbitration.

Arbitration—a dispute resolution procedure in which an independent third party decides and recommends how the disagreement should be resolved. In most union contracts it is the final step of the grievance procedure.

CONTROLS IN STAFFING (HRM)

Performance appraisal is perhaps the most obvious and universal form of control found in the staffing/human resources management function. In general, performance appraisal processes have one or both of two objectives (which may be at odds with one another). The first objective is to provide the organization's managers with information and records that can be used to make decisions about such personnel actions as pay raises, promotions, transfers, training and termination. The second objective is to correct or improve performance by providing the employee with feedback that will help him correct his own performance. Coaching by a supervisor can also help meet this objective.

The performance appraisal process usually results in a written document and a formal interview between the supervisor (rater) and the employee. Both the document and the interview are given the name **performance appraisal**.

A variety of formal performance appraisal methods exist. The most widely used are **graphic rating scales** on which the rater assigns the rated person a value on a scale often done by putting a check mark on a line marked off in intervals. This is done for several traits or types of behavior such as initiative, reliability, attendance, etc.

In the **ranking method**, employees are compared to one another. The rater ranks them in order from best to worst according to some aspect of performance, such as sales volume.

A method recently developed and more popular with researchers than with organizational users is **BARS (behaviorally anchored rating scales)**. BARS requires the rater to describe the employee's behavior by using pre-established descriptions which extensive research has related to effectiveness. BARS focus on objectively observable behaviors instead of traits.

Much more popular, is **Management By Objectives (MBO)** which has a great many varieties. The essence of MBO is that the employee and his supervisor agree, at the start of the rating period, on a number of goals that the employee will try to achieve. The employee is rated at the end of the rating period in terms of the degree to which these goals have been accomplished.

HUMAN ASSET ACCOUNTING

Another aspect of the Control function operating within the staffing function is Human Asset Accounting, a term coined by Rensis Likert. The focus is on how well the human or social side of the entire organization is working. Likert emphasized that the tremendous investment in human resources and the dependence of organizations on them should require objective reporting of the state of those assets both internally to management and externally to investors and other stakeholders. The Survey of Organizations (SOO) developed by associates of Likert at the University of Michigan has been widely used to provide the kind of information about organization functioning, climate, and morale asked for by Human Asset Accounting.

KEY WORDS, PHRASES AND ABBREVIATIONS:

(write out definitions or examples below)

AFL-CIO

application blank

apprenticeship

arbitration

assessment center

association

BARS

benefits

Bona Fide Occupational Qualification (BFOQ)

certification

Civil Rights Act, 1964

collective bargaining

compensation

compensation management

contract

contract administration

contract negotiations

craft (union)

development

disciplinary action

employee inventory chart

employment interview

employment test

equal employment opportunity

Equal Employment Opportunity Commission (EEOC)

Equal Pay Act, 1963

ERiSA

general (union)

grievance

grievance procedure

human resource management

human resource development

industrial (union)

job

job analysis

job description

job evaluation

job rotation

job specification

labor relations

Landrum-Griffin Act

local (union)

manpower planning

mediation

NLRA

NLRB

national (union)

needs assessment

OJT

organizing process (union)

orientation

Occupational Safety and Health Act (OSHA)

performance appraisal

physical examination

recruitment

reference

retirement

selection process

staffing (function)

Taft-Hartley Act

Title VII (Civil Rights Act)

training

uniform guidelines

union

vestibule training

wage and salary administration

Wagner Act

Chapter 4: Sample Questions

1. The attempt to reflect the significant investments involved in acquiring, developing, and maintaining the human resources of the firm is the concern of (the):

   (A) human relations movement
   (B) human-asset accounting
   (C) humanities consultants
   (D) management humanists
   (E) none of the above

2. Which of the following would LEAST likely be of concern to the Human Resources or Personnel Manager:

   (A) Equal Pay Act of 1963
   (B) Occupational Safety and Health Act (1970)
   (C) Employee Retirement Income Security Act (ERISA) 1974
   (D) Environmental Protection Agency regulations
   (E) none of the above (all would be equal concern)

3. A written statement which defines job duties, results expected, and relationship to other jobs is called a:

   (A) job posting
   (B) job referral
   (C) job determination
   (D) job description
   (E) none of the above

4. A person's qualifications to perform various kinds of work would be found in a (an):

   (A) personality survey
   (B) employment test
   (C) personal data sheet
   (D) retirement certificate
   (E) all of the above

5. Which one of the following is NOT a type of interview used in the selection process:

   (A) directive
   (B) non-directive
   (C) fictional
   (D) structured
   (E) none of the above: (all are interview types used in selection)

6. The process which describes how well a person is doing a job is called:

   (A) job performance
   (B) performance appraisal
   (C) assessment center
   (D) compensation management
   (E) job evaluation

7. A type of union that is made up of workers in the same trade or skill such as plumbers or electricians is called a _____ union.

    (A) craft
    (B) general
    (C) industrial
    (D) national
    (E) local

8. The process which tells new employees about the organization's policies, procedures, services, and benefit programs is usually called:

    (A) programmed instruction
    (B) employee training
    (C) apprentice training
    (D) orientation
    (E) confrontation

9. Training methods used in industry include:

    (A) vestibule, classroom, OJT, apprenticeship
    (B) contingency, systems, factorial
    (C) filtering, sequencing, routing
    (D) GANTT, PERT, EOQ
    (E) all of the above

10. The performance appraisal system which attempts to evaluate performance against actual descriptions of effective or ineffective job behaviors is:

    (A) ranking method
    (B) forced-choice method
    (C) trait approach
    (D) PERT
    (E) BARS method

11. The most important and appropriate device to use to find out if a job applicant has the specific skills and knowledge required to perform the job would be a (an):

    (A) aptitude test
    (B) personality test
    (C) achievement test
    (D) Rohrshach test
    (E) intelligence test

Chapter 4: Answers

1. B Human Asset Accounting, a concept originated by Rensis Likert.

2. D The Human Resources Manager would have prime concerns for A, B, and C as part of her job. EPA regulations would typically be more the concern of other departments (e.g., Manufacturing or Marketing).

3. D A job description includes these things.

4. C A personal-data sheet would contain information about the employees job qualifications including training and experience.

5. C Directive, non-directive, and structured are all types of interviews used in selection. The exception, and correct answer, is "C—fictional."

6. B Performance appraisal. Sometimes confused with it is the term "job evaluation" which is the process of determining the money value of a job.

7. A Craft unions are made up of workers in the same skill or craft such as carpenters.

8. D Orientation programs are designed to do these things.

9. A All items in answer A are forms of training.

10. E BARS—behaviorally anchored rating scales.

11. C Achievement tests measure what a person knows or knows how to do. Aptitude tests measure how likely a person is to learn a particular skill or body of information. Personality tests (of which the Rohrshach is one) measure motivations and ways of perceiving. Intelligence tests measure general cognitive abilities.

Chapter 5: Directing/Leading

Directing or leading is the management function of getting people to actually do what needs to be done to carry out plans and achieve goals. It has often been said that leadership breathes life into the organization's structure. To some degree authority remains a hunting license until leadership gets followers to accept it—an idea suggested by Chester Barnard's Acceptance Theory of Authority.

The Acceptance Theory of Authority is the idea that the authority of any communication or command lies in the degree to which the receiver accepts it as legitimate. It is usually associated with Chester Barnard's book The Functions of the Executive.

Directing or leading involves the use of power and influence. One definition of leadership is the ability to influence others to behave in a desired way. A number of different types of power have been distinguished based on the source.

Power—the ability to influence the behavior of others.

Influence—viewed as the essence or equivalent of leadership by some; it is the ability to get others to do something desired by the person doing the influencing.

Legitimate power—is based on position and the authority assigned to that position in the formal organization. In the traditional or classical view, authority originated in ownership and is delegated by the owners to the board of directors, to management, and so forth.

Reward power—is based on the ability of the leader or power-holder to administer rewards or control access to desired goods and services.

Coercive power—is based on the ability to inflict punishment or deprive others of something valued.

Expert power—is based on personal knowledge, skill or competence. Its effects are usually limited to the area of expertise.

Referent power—is based on the followers' liking, admiration, or respect for the power holder or leader. In extreme cases this admiration takes the form of reverence or belief in the leader's prophetic qualities or even divinity. Thus, referent power may blend in to what Max Weber described as charisma or charismatic authority.

LEADERSHIP

Three main approaches to leadership, both its study and its practice, have been 1) trait, 2) behavioral, 3) contingency.

The **trait approach** looks for permanent traits of personality which distinguish leaders from non-leaders or effective leaders from ineffective ones. The trait approach tends to believe that a person must be born with the traits necessary for leadership before he can benefit from leadership training.

The **behavioral approach** emerged in World War II with the focus shifting from traits to what effective leaders did—how they behaved—as opposed to ineffective leaders. Two famous and important programs of leadership research were conducted after World War II at Ohio State University and at the University of Michigan.

The **Ohio State University leadership studies** focused on leadership behavior (as opposed to traits). From them emerged two independent dimensions of leadership behavior: **consideration** and **initiating structure.**

> **Consideration**—leadership behaviors include showing interest in the personal life and well-being of the employee, being warm and friendly, and listening to the employee's ideas.

> **Initiating structure**—involves giving direction and orders, clarifying jobs and roles, explaining objectives and pressuring subordinates for task performance.

The **University of Michigan leadership studies** focused on behaviors that distinguished supervisors of high performing work groups from those of less effective groups. Two dimensions of leader behavior were identified using questionnaires: **employee-centered** and **production-centered** (corresponding roughly to the Ohio State dimensions of consideration and initiating structure). These dimensions were found to be independent of one another and the most effective leaders were found to be fairly high on both dimensions—for them production was important but not all-important. Much of Rensis Likert's Systems 4 theory of management was based on these researches.

> **Employee-centered supervision**—the employee-centered style involves concern for employee well-being and openness to employee suggestions.

> **Production-centered supervision** emphasizes the importance of getting the job done.

Following the trait and behavioral approaches came several **contingency approaches** to leadership.

Contingency approaches to leadership see the effectiveness of any leadership behavior or style as dependent on factors in the situation such as employee characteristics, the nature of the problem, the leader's authority and relation with his subordinates. The contingency approach was developed after trait approaches and behavioral approaches were studied and defined.

TANNENBAUM AND SCHMIDT

One of the first of the contingency or situational approaches was presented by Robert Tannenbaum and Warren Schmidt in a <u>Harvard Business Review</u> article under the title "How to Choose a Leadership Pattern." They suggested a continuum of decision-making styles ranging from **boss-centered** to **subordinate-centered.** At the boss-centered extreme the boss makes the decision by himself and simply tells the subordinates. Other points on the continuum, that is other options for the leader, include: sell the decision to the subordinates; tell the subordinates the decision and ask for questions; present a problem and ask for subordinate ideas; turn the problem over to the subordinates for their decision within specified limits. Finally, at the other extreme from boss-centered is subordinate-centered leadership that involves full delegation of the boss' decision-making authority to the subordinates.

In more general usage, a subordinate-centered or subordinate-oriented leadership style shows concern for the well-being and morale of subordinates as well as encourages their participation in organizational decisions and management.

According to Tannenbaum and Schmidt, whether the leader's style should be boss-centered or subordinate-centered (or in between) depends on the purposes and attitudes of the leader, the nature of the subordinates, and on a variety of factors in the situation, including time pressures.

Two other prominent contingency models of leadership are Fred Fielder's **Contingency Theory of Leadership Effectiveness** and Robert House's **Path-Goal Theory.**

FIEDLER'S CONTINGENCY THEORY

Fiedler's theory examines a large body of research and finds that the effectiveness of a particular leadership style depends on the situation. The leader's style is measured by the **LPC Scale** (LPC stands for least-preferred coworker)—high LPC leaders are relations-oriented, low LPC leaders are task-oriented. Low LPC leaders rate the persons with whom they could work least well in rather negative terms; high LPC leaders rate them much more positively.

The situation is described as favorable or unfavorable to the leader (favorable if the leader has high situational control, unfavorable if control is low). Favorableness is made up of three dimensions: leader-member relations, task-structure, and leader position-power.

Leader-member relations is how well the group members get along with one another and with the leader.

Task structure is whether or not the job is done according to an established plan or routine.

Leader position power is the ability of the leader to hire or fire, recommend promotion, and administer rewards and punishments.

Good relations, a structured task, and high leader position power result in a favorable situation or high control; their opposites result in an unfavorable situation of low control.

Fiedler's central proposition is that groups led by high LPC (relations-oriented) leaders perform best when the situation is one of intermediate favorableness or control; low LPC (task-oriented) leaders do best in situations at the extremes—very favorable or very unfavorable. Leaders, Fiedler believes, can not change their style to fit the situation. Instead, they should learn to change the situation to match their style or seek situations in which their style will work best.

HOUSE'S CONTINGENCY THEORY

House's **Path-Goal Theory** is a contingency form of leadership model which sees the leader's role as helping subordinates to see organizational goals and their payoffs more clearly. The leader clears the employee's path to the goals through coaching, removing obstacles, and the like. What leader behaviors are appropriate depend on the subordinates' motives and personality and the nature of the task. In a routine, repetitive task the manager should provide **supportive leadership**; **directive leadership** would be appropriate when the job is complex, non-routine or involves new elements. Other leader behaviors in the path-goal model are **participative** and **achievement-oriented.**

MOTIVATION

Motivation is the processes by which behavior is energized, aroused, directed and kept going. To influence others, to lead or direct, requires an understanding of human motivation. We will briefly summarize key ideas from seven motivational theories prominent in the management literature. These are:

Maslow's Need Hierarchy Theory

Herzberg's Two-Factor (Motivator-Hygiene) Theory

Reinforcement Theory

McClelland's work on Need for Achievement, Need for Power, and Need for Affiliation

Goal Setting Theory

Expectancy Theory

Equity Theory

Need Hierarchy Theory is Maslow's theory of motivation which arranges human needs into five groups in a **hierarchy of pre-potency.** Lower order needs must be satisfied before higher needs are active. A satisfied need is no longer a motivator of behavior. The need immediately above it on the hierarchy then becomes the motivator.

> The lowest level of needs in Maslow's hierarchy are **physiological needs** like hunger and thirst.

> **Safety needs** are those grouped at the second level from the bottom of the hierarchy, above physiological needs and below love or social needs. Safety needs include needs for physical safety and health as well as for predictable life and work conditions and job security.

> **Social needs**—called love by Maslow—come into play only after physiological and security needs have been met. They involve opportunities for friendship, conversation, understanding supervisors, and pleasant coworkers.

> **Esteem needs** are the fourth and next highest level of need. They include needs for recognition and respect from others, as well as self-respect.

> At the top of Maslow's hierarchy are **self-actualization needs**—to become what you are capable of becoming.

The Maslow need hierarchy was introduced into management thinking by Douglas McGregor's book **The Human Side of Enterprise** in which Theory Y essentially summarized much of Maslow's view of human nature and motivation. (See page 64, "Management Philosophies.")

Two-Factor Theory of Motivation is another name for Herzberg's motivator-hygiene theory which asserts that motivators or satisfiers lead to extraordinary job performance whereas hygiene factors or dissatisfiers simply keep the employee showing up for work and doing the minimum needed to hold his/her job. This provides the logic underlying Herzberg's orthodox job enrichment, which enhances employee motivation and satisfaction by building more **motivators** (e.g., responsibilities) into the job.

> **Motivator factors** in Herzberg's two-factor, motivator-hygiene theory, are factors such as recognition, responsibility, achievement, professional growth and development, and the work itself. They are intrinsic and part of the job content. Motivators are also called satisfiers. They lead to effort and creative work beyond the bare minimum caused by hygiene factors.

> **Hygiene factors** are things extrinsic to the work found in the job context such as working conditions (rather than the work itself), interpersonal relations, company policy and administration, supervision, pay and benefits. All these simply keep the employee from quitting—they do **NOT** motivate exceptional performance.

Reinforcement theory refers generally to learning theory and similar behavioristic approaches to understanding and controlling behavior. The basic ideas stem from the work of B.F. Skinner on operant conditioning. Fundamental to the theory is that behavior followed by reinforcement tends to be repeated—Thorndike's **Law of Effect.** Reinforcement theory and behaviorism avoid the use of internal mental or motivational processes. It is thought that behavior can be fully explained and controlled by use of objective observable behaviors and events: stimuli, responses and contingencies of reinforcement following the response.

Positive reinforcement is any event or change which follows the behavior and increases the likelihood that the behavior will occur again in the same circumstances. Most frequent positive reinforcers are things desired by or pleasant to the individual whose behavior is being reinforced.

Negative reinforcement is the stopping of pain. Whatever behavior achieves or precedes this result is reinforced. Thus negative reinforcement involves reinforcement by the termination of a pre-existing pain—basically what is involved in extortion.

Punishment is an aversive or unpleasant event that follows a behavior. It has the effect over time of decreasing the frequency of the behavior (assuming the behavior is not continuing to lead to reinforcement or reward).

Extinction. In learning theory/reinforcement theory, behavior that is not followed by any noticeable result or reinforcement tends to disappear, is weakened, or is less likely to reoccur. This process is called extinction and may be accidental or deliberate.

Behavior modification is the application to problems of industrial management (worker motivation) of the reinforcement theory, particularly positive reinforcement and the principles of operant or instrumental learning of B. F. Skinner.

McCLELLAND'S NEEDS THEORY

In a study conducted by David McClelland and his associates it was found that the need for **achievement, power** and **affiliation** are especially relevant to organizational behavior.

Achievement motivation. The need for achievement is an important motive that is particularly relevant to business because it is strong in entrepreneurs, independent businessmen, outside salesmen, and many managers. The person high in need for achievement strives for challenging goals of moderate difficulty, wants concrete and immediate feedback, and prefers work situations where he/she is solely responsible for the results.

Power. The need for power is defined as the need to have an impact on others and a concern for getting control of the means of influence and control. There are two kinds: an exploitative, self-oriented power need which is contrasted with socialized power that is used to benefit others and involves a large element of self-control.

The need for **affiliation** is the desire for warm, friendly relationships—similar to Maslow's needs category of love and belonging.

Equity theory proposes that people try to maintain or establish an equality between their own ratio of what they put in to a job versus what they get out of it and the ratio of inputs to outcomes of a comparison person. They try to maintain an equation that looks something like this: I/O (self) = I/O (other).

If the ratios are equal the comparison is seen as fair or equitable. If unequal, the person is motivated to restore equity in any of several ways or to get out of the situation.

Goal setting theory—a group of propositions and supporting research which indicate that people work harder/better to achieve goals that are: specific rather than vague, general or undefined; that are accepted by them; and that are challenging rather than easy.

Expectancy theory—a cognitive model of motivation according to the formula: $E = (E)(I)(V)$. This says that effort (or motivation) is the product of the desirability or valence (V) of the final outcomes; the believed likelihood that effort will lead to effective performance (expectancy, E); and the subjective probability that effective performance will lead to the final outcomes (instrumentality, I). A number of versions of the model exist.

MANAGEMENT PHILOSOPHIES

Several management writers and researchers have attempted to describe broad systems of managerial leadership which combine philosophies of human nature and motivation with conceptions of the most effective ways of structuring and leading organizations. Many of these systems advocate participative approaches to management. **Participation** means employee involvement in decisions about work-related matters.

Participative management gets employee involvement in decision-making and the direction and control of work. Forms range from consultation (in which employee opinions about changes are asked) to autonomous work groups where employees essentially manage and are responsible for their own work.

Two views that have had a strong influence on management thinking are Douglas McGregor's **Theory X and Theory Y** and Rensis Likert's **System 4 Management.**

Theory X; Theory Y are contrasting views and sets of assumptions held by managers and their resultant management tactics. Described by Douglas McGregor in The Human Side of Enterprise, traditional management (Theory X) viewed man as basically lazy, without initiative, and incapable of responsibility, preferring to do as little work as possible. This necessitates external threats or incentives to get people to work. To this McGregor contrasted Theory Y (essentially borrowed wholesale from Abraham Maslow) which is the view that motivation is internal, that the desire to work is as natural as the desire to play, that people can accept responsibility and exercise self-control in pursuit of goals with which they identify. Satisfied motives no longer motivate behavior, and workers in advanced countries today have motives at a higher level (e.g., esteem needs) than did their forefathers who were concerned with survival.

System 4 is a collegial and participative model of management described by Rensis Likert as involving the principle of supportive relationships, an overlapping group form of organization, and high performance goals. System 4 was at the right hand end of a scale which began with System 1, an exploitative, authoritarian model of management.

STRESS AND PERFORMANCE

An aspect of motivation which leadership must manage is stress. **Stress** is the response or reaction to adaptive demands on the individual. These demands are called **stressors**. Stressors may be physical (heat, cold, toxic chemicals) or psychological (threats, role conflict, frustration).

A major organizational source of stress is **role conflict**—different and conflicting expectations of job behavior held, for instance, by coworkers, superiors and subordinates. (A **role** is the set of behaviors expected of the occupant of a position in the organization.)

Most research indicates that as the level of stress increases, the quality of performance decreases. However, some authorities argue that up to some optimum level performance gets better with increasing stress and then deteriorates.

NAMES TO REMEMBER:

Chester Barnard	-	author of <u>Functions of the Executive</u>; acceptance theory of authority
Frederick Herzberg	-	two-factor (motivator-hygiene) theory of motivation, a pioneer in job enrichment
Fred Fiedler	-	contingency model of leadership effectiveness, measures leadership style in terms of LPC (High LPC is relations-oriented, Low LPC is task-oriented). Whether High or Low LPC leader results in an effective group depends on the degree of situational control or favorableness.
Robert House	-	path-goal theory of leadership, a contingency model
Rensis Likert	-	System 4 theory of management, a participative model
Abraham Maslow	-	need hierarchy model of human motivation
David McClelland	-	need for achievement, need for affiliation, need for power, more recently developed the Leader Motivation Profile (LMP)
Douglas McGregor	-	Theory X, Theory Y
B.F. Skinner	-	a radical behaviorist, associated with operant conditioning, reinforcement theory, behavior modification

KEY WORDS, PHRASES AND ABBREVIATIONS

(write out definitions or examples below)

acceptance theory of authority

achievement (need for)

achievement motivation theory

affiliation (need for)

boss-centered leadership

coercive power

consideration

contingency models of leadership

employee-centered supervision

equity theory

esteem needs

expectancy theory

expert power

extinction

goal-setting theory

hygiene factors

influence

initiating structure

legitimate power

need hierarchy theory

Ohio State University leadership studies

motivation

negative reinforcement

participation

participative management

path-goal theory

production-centered supervision

position power

positive reinforcement

power

power (need for)

punishment

referent power

reinforcement theory

relationship-oriented (leadership style)

reward power

role

role conflict

safety needs

stress

stressors

subordinate-centered leadership

System 4

task-oriented (leadership style)

Theory X

Theory Y

two-factor theory of motivation

University of Michigan leadership studies

1. In its broadest sense, the management of people so as to achieve objectives is what is involved in:

    (A) planning
    (B) organizing
    (C) directing or leading
    (D) decision-making
    (E) controlling

2. Susan Jones delegates a lot, gives her subordinates plenty of authority and responsibility, and involves them in making important company decisions. Susan seems to be:

    (A) nuts
    (B) using Theory Y
    (C) using Theory X
    (D) all of the above
    (E) none of the above

3. A need for control or influence over others or wanting to have an impact or make an impression define the need for:

    (A) achievement
    (B) affiliation
    (C) power
    (D) self-control
    (E) none of the above

4. According to Frederick Herzberg's "two-factor" theory of work motivation:

    (A) motivators include working conditions, supervision, company policies
    (B) hygiene factors include factors intrinsic to the job and the work content
    (C) satisfaction and dissatisfaction are opposite ends of a single dimension
    (D) all of the above
    (E) none of the above

5. Operant conditioning or instrumental learning is associated with all of the following EXCEPT:

    (A) B.F. Skinner
    (B) Frederick Taylor
    (C) behavior modification
    (D) Law of Effect
    (E) positive reinforcement

6. According to the Law of Effect, behavior followed by a satisfying state or a reward, tends to be:

(A) inefficient
(B) inappropriate
(C) omitted
(D) repeated
(E) none of the above

7. According to the expectancy model of motivation:

(A) effort or motivation depends on all of at least three separate variables
(B) "valence" is defined as the desirability or undesirability of an outcome or consequence of effort
(C) "instrumentality" is the anticipated likelihood that a particular performance will lead to a particular reward or punishment
(D) all of the above
(E) none of the above

8. The importance given to leadership in modern management thinking relates back to:

(A) Attila the Hun
(B) The Hawthorne Studies
(C) Frederick Taylor and Scientific Management
(D) Adam Smith
(E) Harry Truman

9. The Ohio State and University of Michigan researches on leadership focused on the leader's _____ .

(A) behaviors
(B) education
(C) personality
(D) traits
(E) none of the above

10. In the University of Michigan leadership research, the dimensions studied were called (1) _____ and (2) _____.

(A) (1) dimension 1, (2) dimension 2
(B) (1) Theory X, (2) Theory Y
(C) (1) proactive, (2) reactive
(D) (1) employee-centered, (2) production-centered
(E) none of the above

11. Leader style in Fiedler's Theory is measured by the LPC scale. High LPC leaders are (1) _____ whereas low LPC leaders are said to be (2) _____.

(A) (1) work-oriented, (2) play-oriented
(B) (1) success-oriented, (2) security-oriented
(C) (1) achievement-oriented, (2) profit-oriented
(D) (1) relations-oriented, (2) task-oriented
(E) none of the above

12. The continuum of leader decision-making behaviors (outlined by Tannenbaum and Schmidt) ranges from (1) _____ at one extreme to (2) _____ at the other extreme.

    (A) (1) consultation, (2) voting
    (B) (1) unilateral decision, (2) one man rule
    (C) (1) boss centered leadership, (2) subordinate-centered leadership
    (D) (1) efficient styles, (2) inefficient styles
    (E) none of the above

Chapter 5: Answers

1. C   Directing or leading. (Some would argue that this is the definition of management.)

2. B   Managers who act on the basis of Theory Y assume that people can and want to accept responsibility and will work toward organizational objectives.

3. C   This defines the need for power as outlined by psychologist David McClelland.

4. E   None of the above. According to Herzberg, working conditions, supervision, and policies are "hygiene factors." Motivator factors, like achievement and responsibility, are intrinsic to the job. Satisfaction is a separate dimension from dissatisfaction.

5. B   The exception is Frederick Taylor of Scientific Management fame. B.F. Skinner developed the laws of operant conditioning. The application of operant conditioning principles to industry (and other practical concerns) has been given the name "behavior modification."

6. D   According to Thorndike's "Law of Effect," behavior that leads to satisfaction is repeated. Part II said that behavior followed by unpleasant consequences tends to disappear.

7. D   The "expectancy model" (or expectancy-valence theory) proposes that motivation or effort is the product of "expectancy", "instrumentality," and "valence."

8. B   The Hawthorne studies showed that social psychological factors such as morale, group norms, and leadership could affect production just as much as physical working conditions.

9. B   Behaviors. The Ohio State leader behaviors were "consideration" and "initiating structure."

10. D   Employee-centered and production-centered leader behaviors corresponding to the Ohio State "consideration" and "initiating structure."

11. D   In Fiedler's Contingency Theory, high LPC leaders are relations-oriented, low LPC are task-oriented.

12. C   Boss-centered to subordinate-centered.

Chapter 6: Control And Operational Aspects

Controlling is the management function that insures that performance agrees with plans and if not, takes corrective action.

The **control process** includes three steps: establishes performance standards; measures performance; and produces feedback measurement information for corrective action or reinforcement.

Measurable standards/goals/objectives are requirements for and steps in the controlling process. They are derived from plans.

Measurement/observation is a step in the controlling process in which performance is measured or observed reliably in order to compare it to a standard. Measurement and observation are also part of the problem-solving and decision-making process. If the observation step of the control process reveals a variance from a standard, this initiates a problem-solving process.

Feedback is information given to a person or organization about performance. In the control process, feedback of measurements of performance allows for reinforcement or corrective action.

Characteristics of effective controls: timely and relevant; strategic; desired and accepted; descriptive and objective versus moralistic, threatening, or punitive.

An important control concept is expressed in the **exception principle**—this is the idea that routine problems covered by established policies and procedures should be handled at lower levels of the organization; exceptions should be dealt with by higher levels. This is similar to **management by exception**—that management should give priority attention to performance or action that deviates from the plan or fails to meet expectations.

KINDS OF CONTROLS

Pre-controls are actions taken before the performance of an individual or organization occurs to try to insure it will go as planned. Inspection of parts prior to assembly is one example, training is another.

Concurrent controls make sure actions are going according to plan, while the actions are being done—NOW—as opposed to pre-control and post control. Direct supervision is an example.

Post controls are actions taken after the event or performance. Examples include audits, postmortems, and reviews of actions or plans.

Over time we can also distinguish among types of controls on the basis of their frequency. **Constant controls** are in place and at work all of the time to keep actions in line with plans. Examples include self-control, group norms and close supervision. Many mechanical or automatic controls are of this type.

Occasional controls are actions, observations, or procedures which occur from time to time, such as occasional plant tours by the superintendent and random unannounced inspections or audits. **Periodic controls** involve observation and measurement of performance at specified time intervals—daily, monthly, quarterly, etc.

Another important distinction between controls is whether they are **external** or **internal.**

External controls from an individual psychological point of view involve a second person to be the supervisor of the first person's behavior. From an organizational point of view, as in the form of the **external audit,** the term external controls refers to the inspection and verification of an organization's finances or other procedures by an outside, independent firm or person.

Internal controls are from a psychological viewpoint the same thing as self-control: the individual or group tries to keep its own performance in line with standards which have been internalized—accepted as its own.

Theory X and **Theory Y**. In The Human Side of Enterprise, Douglas McGregor describes two contrasting sets of assumptions about human nature held by managers and different underlying approaches to management. Theory X assumes man is basically lazy, unwilling to accept responsibility and requires external motivation and control. Theory Y assumes that people are motivated from within, that they can enjoy work as much as play, that they can be responsible, and that they are capable of self control.

INVENTORY CONTROL

Inventory refers to the goods, materials, and equipment kept for sale or use. **Inventory control** is the process and procedures for insuring that inventory use, security, and costs are within planned limits.

The **ABC inventory system** is an approach to inventory control which assigns inventory items to three groups in terms of dollar value or criticality. Group A—worth as a whole about 70-80% of total inventory—receives the greatest expenditure of control effort and expense. Group B gets less attention than A but more attention than C. Group C, which may account for less than 10% of total inventory value gets the least attention.

Safety stock is the amount of inventory needed to be kept on hand so that production, sales, or other activities can go on despite unexpected contingencies (e.g., a stop in deliveries).

ECONOMIC ORDER QUANTITY

An approach to inventory control and to the analysis of inventory control problems, **economic order quantity (EOQ)** is the name given to both the method and the key term or quantity which it yields. EOQ is the quantity that should be purchased in order to keep total inventory costs (carrying costs plus ordering costs) at the lowest level. (See Figure 6-1.)

Ordering costs, in the EOQ method for analyzing and controlling inventory costs, are the costs of getting materials into inventory. They include administrative costs per order, transportation, cost per item, etc. As Figure 6-1 shows, ordering costs decrease as the size of the order increases.

Carrying costs, in the EOQ analysis, are the expenses of keeping inventory on hand before it is used or sold. They increase as the order size gets bigger.

Total inventory costs are the sum of carrying costs plus ordering costs for any quantity ordered. The EOQ is the point at which total costs are lowest, in Figure 6-1, where the ordering costs line crosses the carrying costs line.

ECONOMIC ORDER QUANTITY (EOQ)

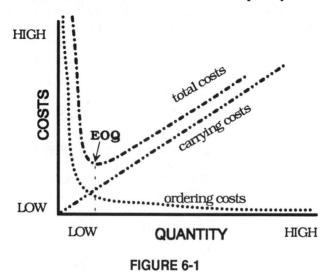

FIGURE 6-1

JUST-IN-TIME (JIT) AND ZERO INVENTORY (ZI)

The **just-in-time (JIT)** inventory system is a Japanese-developed method for reducing inventory by shifting responsibility to the supplier. The supplier must deliver needed goods in small or exactly needed amounts to the place in the production process (or other location) where it is needed, at or near the time when it will actually be used.

Zero inventory (ZI) is a goal under the JIT inventory system in which all carrying costs are born by the supplier and the manufacturer has on hand only enough to meet immediate production needs. Low inventories and short production runs help promote rapid detection and correction of defects.

ACCEPTANCE SAMPLING

Acceptance sampling is a control procedure in which a small number of items (a sample) from a production lot are inspected. If a predetermined number of items in the sample fails to meet the standard, the entire lot may be inspected or rejected. Sampling standards of acceptance may be by attributes (go/no-go) or by variables (within a specified range).

Statistical acceptance sampling is the use of statistical sampling theory, based on probabilities, to determine the size sample required to insure a given degree of quality (for example, only one defect per 1000) with a specified level of confidence (e.g., 95% probability). In general, the more certain you want to be that the characteristics of the whole lot inspected are the same as the values found in the sample, the larger the sample must be.

MASTER PLANNING

The subject of inventory control as an integral part of the overall production process is too complex to be discussed here. We will, however, introduce several of the terms and concepts in use.

Materials Requirements Planning (MRP) is a term in use before 1980. It refers to the system for planning and controlling production activities, including material needs, and other factors as well. Another name for this overall approach is **PIPC** or **production and inventory planning and control**. PIPC was used to describe the combined materials and manufacturing planning systems which eventually led to MRP II.

Manufacturing Resources Planning (MRP II) is a complex approach to production and inventory planning developed in the early 1980's that attempts to include input from ALL functional areas in the planning process (e.g., from marketing, from engineering, from finance). It starts with an overall strategic plan and master production schedule.

Part of MRP II is **capacity requirements planning (CRP)**, a calculation of restrictions on production capacity imposed by machines and labor.

FINANCIAL CONTROLS

A **budget** is a plan for the expenditure or use of resources (and often results expected) stated in quantitative terms, usually dollars.

A **capital budget** is the planned spending for equipment and buildings.

An **operating budget** includes projected expenses for labor, materials, rent utilities, and other non-capital items.

Variable budgets permit budgeted amounts to vary as a function of changes in such things as sales, weather, etc. Sales expenses, for example, would be allowed to increase and more salespeople could be hired if sales increased.

Zero-based budgeting is an approach which requires that all budget items be justified in their entirety each year.

Financial statements used in the controlling function include the **balance sheet** and the **earnings statement.** A balance sheet shows assets balanced against liabilities and owners' equity. An earnings statement (also called a **P&L or profit-and-loss statement**) shows revenues (income), costs of goods sold and expenses, and net profit or net loss for the specified time period.

Financial ratios are control devices involving the division of one measure (of activity or resources) by another—for example, sales/total assets (asset turnover ratio—an **activity ratio**). The four main groups of financial ratios are: 1) liquidity, 2) activity, 3) profitability and 4) leverage.

> **Liquidity ratios** measure the ability to raise cash and pay debts. One is the **current ratio** defined as current assets/current liabilities. Another is the **quick ratio** which is the ability to meet an emergency.

> **Activity ratios** measure the efficiency of use of resources. They include: revenues/assets, accounts receivable/revenues, sales/inventory, inventory turnover ratio (number of times inventory is sold in a given time period).

> **Profitability ratios** include earnings per share, return on total assets, return on stockholders' investment, and return on total assets.

> **Leverage ratios** measure the degree of debt. The debt-equity ratio is defined as total liabilities/total equities. The same idea is the debt to total assets ratio (debt/total assets).

SCHEDULING AND PROGRAM PLANNING AND CONTROL

The **Gantt chart** is a scheduling and control device invented by Henry L. Gantt, an associate of Frederick Taylor. Activities, machine use, and steps in a project are listed from top to bottom on the left side of the vertical axis. Time (usually dates) is shown running from left to right on the horizontal axis. The planned or scheduled time for an activity is shown as a horizontal bar running from the date for the start of the activity to its end. An example of a Gantt chart is shown as Figure 6-2.

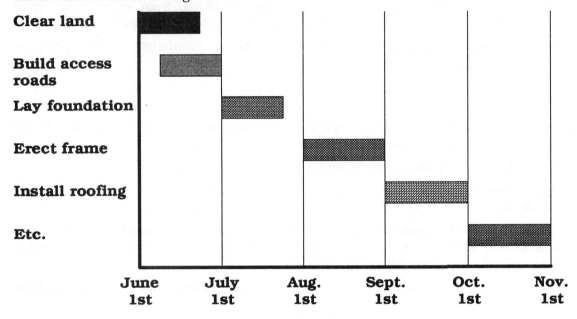

GANTT CHART
(Hypothetical Construction Project)

FIGURE 6-2

A logical progression from the Gantt chart was to **network-methods** like PERT or CPM which display a project or program as interconnected groupings of series of activities for purposes of analysis, planning, and control.

Program Evaluation and Review Technique (PERT) is a planning and control method which displays an entire project as a number of activities and sequences of activities all connected as a network. A much simplified example of a PERT chart is given in Figure 6-3.

PERT CHART

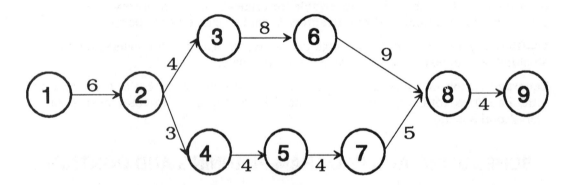

EXPECTED TIMES are shown above the arrows as the number of days required for each activity. The CRITICAL PATH is through events 1, 2, 3, 6, 8 and 9 requiring a total of 31 days. The path through events 1, 2, 4, 5, 7, 8 and 9 requires a total of 26 days.

FIGURE 6-3

CPM stands for **critical path method**—variants of PERT which, like it, show the various steps of a project (activities and events) and the times estimated for completion. The longest connected sequence of activities, or critical path, requires careful managing.

In a PERT or CPM network, **activities** are the work which takes place and the time consumed between events (from start to finish). The PERT chart shows estimated times for each activity.

Events in a PERT or CPM network are the start or end of an activity. Events do not consume time.

The **critical path** in a PERT or CPM network is the series of activities which requires the greatest total amount of time for completion of the entire sequence.

OPERATIONS RESEARCH METHODS

Operations research was originally developed during World War II by interdisciplinary teams of scientists and mathematicians who used scientific methods to analyze and solve practical operational problems. For example, determining the best method to search for a submarine. Operations research subsequently developed into an applied branch of mathematics and a body of quantitative approaches to management decision-making.

Probably the most widely used of the operations research methods is **linear programming.** Others are **probability analysis** (as in a payoff matrix), **queuing theory**, and **simulation**.

> **Simulation** is a technique for imitating operating conditions to see what happens when changes are made.
>
> **Queuing theory** is a quantitative technique for determining the best trade-off between increasing costly service facilities and keeping users (customers, employees, equipment) waiting. It is also called **waiting-line theory**. (In England, a waiting-line is called a queue.)
>
> **Linear programming** is an operations research or quantitative technique useful in planning. It permits a systematic comparison of alternatives to determine which mix will best achieve some objective which can be quantified or minimize some cost. Examples would be scheduling arrangements among machines, expenditures for different kinds of equipment, mixes of components in fertilizer or cattle feed, or of media in an advertising campaign.

STATISTICAL PROCESS CONTROL AND QUALITY CIRCLES

Statistical process control uses sample values and **upper and lower control limits** (UCL's and **LCL**'s) which are the extremes that the sample values may have if the production process is working the way it is supposed to and is **in control**. Statistical process control is a central part of the Deming approach to quality control: if the process is in control, the product does not have to be inspected for quality.

Quality control is a sub-discipline within the production management area concerned with developing and applying techniques for producing goods free of defects and maintaining the reliability of production processes.

Quality Circles (also called **quality control** or **QC circles**) are a Japanese-developed method for achieving a high degree of worker involvement and commitment—that is, for enhancing self-control. Quality circles are small groups of hourly workers trained in data collection and analysis methods who detect and define problems and propose solutions to them. They are taught to use statistical process control methods.

MANAGEMENT INFORMATION SYSTEMS (MIS)

A **management information system (MIS)** is an arrangement of people, procedures, machinery, and usually electronic computers that are used to provide timely and relevant information to various managers.

Information processing is the manipulation of data, usually assisted by electronic computers, to produce information which is usable in making enterprise decisions.

Data are numbers which represent things, people, events or, transactions. Data is not the same thing as information. The **processing system(s)**—a sub-system of an MIS—processes data and transactions, transforming them into information. **Information** is statements about quantities or relationships drawn from data by processing. It has meaning for the user.

Decision support systems (DSS) permit decision-makers to get information fast enough to use in a real-world context. **Management reporting systems** (also known simply as reporting systems) provide the information system support for **routine** (**programmed** or **structured**) decisions. **Unstructured** decisions also called unprogrammed or non-routine decisions, are those for which the decision-maker does not know in advance the information that is needed, the correct procedure to follow, the alternative courses of action, or the criteria to use. An objective of decision support systems is to support such unstructured decisions. **Structured decisions** are those more-or-less routine programmed decisions usually made by lower level executives in which the information needs, steps to be followed, and criteria for judgment are all well established. Structured decisions are supported by management reporting systems.

The **transaction reporting system** of the MIS processes the data of such actions as deposits, withdrawals, orders, payments, and returns which are called **transactions.**

In a **computer system** the **hardware** will include an **input unit** (keyboard), a **central processing unit** (CPU), **storage units** (drive, disk, tape), and **output units** (printer, modem). The programs of instructions that control the operations performed by the hardware are called **software**.

NAMES TO REMEMBER:

W. Edward Deming
- American statistician and production expert who influenced Japanese production/management and particularly the use of statistical process control and Quality Control Circles. Many of his ideas—particularly statistical process control—have recently been widely introduced in American industry.

Henry L. Gantt
- an associate of Frederick Taylor in the Scientific Management movement. He is best known today for the Gantt Chart which he designed. It is still a useful scheduling, planning and control tool.

KEY WORDS, PHRASES AND ABBREVIATIONS:

(write out definitions or examples below)

ABC inventory system

activities

activity ratios

balance sheet

budget

capital budget

carrying costs

concurrent control

constant controls

control/controlling (function)

control limits

control process

criteria/characteristics for effective controls

CPM

critical path

capacity requirements planning (CRP)

current ratio

data

decision support systems (DSS)

earnings statement

economic order quantity (EOQ)

events

exception principle

external controls

feedback

financial ratios

Gantt chart

information

information processing

internal control

JIT

just-in-time inventory system (JIT)

leverage ratios

liquidity ratios

linear programming

management information systems (MIS)

management reporting systems

MIS

Materials Requirements Planning (MRP)

Manufacturing Resources Planning (MRP II)

measurable standards/goals/objectives

measurement/observation

network methods

occasional controls

operating budget

operations research

ordering costs

periodic controls

pre-control

post-control

Program Evaluation Review Technique (PERT)

profit and loss statement

profitability ratios

processing systems

Production and Inventory Planning and Control (PIPC)

quality control

Quality Circles (QC circles)

queuing theory

safety stock

self-control

simulation

software

statistical acceptance sampling

statistical process control

structured decisions

total inventory costs

transaction reporting system

Theory X, Theory Y

unstructured decision

variable budget

zero-based budget

zero inventory (ZI)

Chapter 6: Sample Questions

1. In terms of frequency of occurrence (how often they are applied), controls are classified as:

   (A) external, internal, environmental
   (B) preliminary, extraordinary, supplementary
   (C) credible, incredible, calculable
   (D) constant, periodic, occasional
   (E) imaginary, concrete, abstract

2. At the opposite end of the continuum from external control would be:

   (A) just-in-time control
   (B) ordinary control
   (C) self-control
   (D) hierarchical control
   (E) extraordinary control

3. A work group norm for high levels of production would be an example of what kind of control?

   (A) continuous
   (B) occasional
   (C) periodic
   (D) ad hoc
   (E) just-in-time

4. An American whose name is associated with Japanese quality control, Quality Circles, and statistical process control is:

   (A) W. Edwards Deming
   (B) DeWitt Clinton
   (C) Douglas MacArthur
   (D) Henri Fayol
   (E) Peter Drucker

5. In statistical acceptance sampling, it is generally true that the more certain you want to be that the characteristics of the entire production lot are very similar or identical to those calculated from the sample (assuming random sampling):

   (A) the smaller the sample must be
   (B) the larger the sample must be
   (C) the more objective the sample must be
   (D) the better informed the sample must be
   (E) the less appropriate is the use of random sampling

6. In quality control of machine gun cartridges, in which cartridges are fired in a machine gun to see if they are good, it would make sense to:

   (A) insist on testing 100% of cartridges produced
   (B) select 5% of cartridges produced for testing
   (C) select a number of cartridges sufficient to guarantee peace in our time
   (D) randomly select enough for testing that the probability of having duds in batches accepted is known and is acceptably low
   (E) discard (refuse to accept) a batch in which a single dud is found, following a procedure of selecting from near the exact center of each case of finished cartridges

7. On a Gantt chart the vertical axis would list or show (1)_____, while the horizontal axis would show (2)_____.

   (A) (1) dollars expended, (2) quantity sold
   (B) (1) activities, (2) time
   (C) (1) quantities in production, (2) dollars committed
   (D) (1) volume, (2) variable costs
   (E) (1) vertical forecasts, (2) horizontal forecasts

8. Moving from left to right on a PERT chart we go from (1)_____ to the (2)_____.

   (A) (1) lowest expenditures or costs, (2) highest expenditures or costs
   (B) (1) start of a project, (2) completion of a project
   (C) (1) estimate of a budget, (2) budget review
   (D) (1) least complex technologically, (2) most sophisticated technologically
   (E) (1) higher costs, (2) lower costs

9. Linear programming methods might appropriately be used to determine:

   (A) the best mix of media in a political campaign
   (B) the mix of products that will best meet some marketing objective
   (C) how payroll budget can best be used to hire staff to meet organizational responsibilities
   (D) least costly allocation of production runs of different products among machines
   (E) all of the above

10. Determining the best balance between costs of waiting for service and costs of increasing service facilities would be an appropriate use of:

    (A) ABC method
    (B) Fayol's Bridge
    (C) break-even analysis
    (D) the exception principle
    (E) Queuing theory

Chapter 6: Answers

1. D Constant, periodic, occasional

2. C Self-control (internal control)

3. A Continuous—group pressure for production may not be constant, but it's always there.

4. A W. Edwards Deming

5. B Sample size determines the amount of error in estimating a population value (a parameter), such as the number of duds in a production run. The less error you are willing to accept, the larger the sample you have to pay for. All of the above assumes random sampling.

6. D You want an acceptably low proportion of duds, and you want to know how probable (or unlikely) it is that this could be exceeded if the sample meets the standard.

7. B Activities are listed from top to bottom while time for the activities to occur is shown from left to right horizontally.

8. B From start to completion.

9. E All of the above.

10. E Queuing theory or waiting-line theory would be appropriate.

Answer Sheets

The following pages are copies* of the actual answer sheet you will use when you take a CLEP examination. The information requested must be filled in so that it can be read by a person and also by a computer. This means on page 1 and 2 of the answer sheet you will blacken the circle which has the same letter or number that appears at the top of that column. When you work in the test section, you will blacken the number you have chosen as the correct answer to the question.

With item Number 8, if you do not know the code number of the institution where you wish to have your scores sent, put four 9's in the spaces provided and indicate the name and address of the school. Enter four 0's if you wish to have your scores sent only to yourself.

It is important for you to understand the answer sheet <u>before</u> you go to take the test! Use it when you take your sample test.

SOME TIPS TO REMEMBER WHEN USING A SEPARATE ANSWER SHEET

1. Be **sure** you blacken the entire circle provided for your answer.

2. Be **sure** to put your answers at the proper place on the answer sheet. If you are answering question 30, be **sure** you record your answer at number 30 on the answer sheet.

3. Do **not** put any extra marks on your answer sheet. It may cause the question to be marked incorrect.

4. Be **sure** you record only **one** answer for each question. If you wish to change an answer, be **sure** you erase your first answer completely.

5. Use #2 lead pencils for the multiple choice answers. Use a ball point pen when writing the essay.

COLLEGE-LEVEL EXAMINATION PROGRAM of the College Board
ANSWER SHEET FOR NATIONAL ADMINISTRATIONS — PAGE 1

Use only a soft lead (No. 2) pencil. Be sure each mark is dark and completely fills the intended oval. Erase any errors and stray marks completely.

1. YOUR NAME Omit spaces, hyphens, apostrophes, and Jr. or II.

Last Name — first 12 letters   First Name — first 8 letters   M.I.

2. DATE OF BIRTH

Month	Day	Year
① Jan.		
② Feb.	⓪	⓪
③ Mar.	①	①
④ Apr.	②	②
⑤ May	③	③
⑥ Jun.	④	④
⑦ Jul.	⑤	⑤
⑧ Aug.	⑥	⑥
⑨ Sep.	⑦	⑦
⑩ Oct.	⑧	⑧
⑪ Nov.	⑨	⑨
⑫ Dec.		

3. SEX

Male ①
Female ②

4. SOCIAL SECURITY NUMBER (Optional)

5. CURRENT EDUCATIONAL LEVEL

① High School
② High School Graduate
③ College Freshman
④ College Sophomore
⑤ College Junior
⑥ College Senior
⑦ College Graduate

6. ETHNIC GROUP (Optional) How do you describe yourself?

① American Indian, Eskimo or Aleut
② Black, Afro-American or Negro
③ Mexican American or Chicano
④ Oriental or Asian-American
⑤ Puerto Rican-American
⑥ Other Hispanic or Latin American
⑦ White or Caucasian
⑧ Other

7. TEST CENTER CODE NUMBER

Enter the code number in these boxes.

8. SCORE REPORT RECIPIENT

*Enter the Institution Code Number

Blacken the corresponding oval below each box

Institution Name and Location (Print)

Institution Name

City

State

*If you do not have the code number for the institution you want to receive your reports, enter 9999.

9. FEES PAID   See Admission Form.

Examination Fee......................... $

Special Administration Fee (Fee is $10.)......................... $

Total Paid .... $

Blacken the corresponding oval below each box. →

10. TOTAL NUMBER OF EXAMINATIONS YOU ARE GOING TO TAKE AT THIS ADMINISTRATION.

○ 1   ○ 4   ○ 7   ○ 10
○ 2   ○ 5   ○ 8   ○ more than 10
○ 3   ○ 6   ○ 9

11. SIGNATURE AND DATE

I accept the conditions set forth in the *Registration Guide* concerning the administration of the tests and reporting of scores.

Today's Date:

DO NOT WRITE IN THIS BOX, FOR ETS USE ONLY.

DO NOT BACK FOLD THIS ANSWER SHEET.

I.N. 202853-185VV127P100

12. YOUR MAILING ADDRESS

Number and Street

City

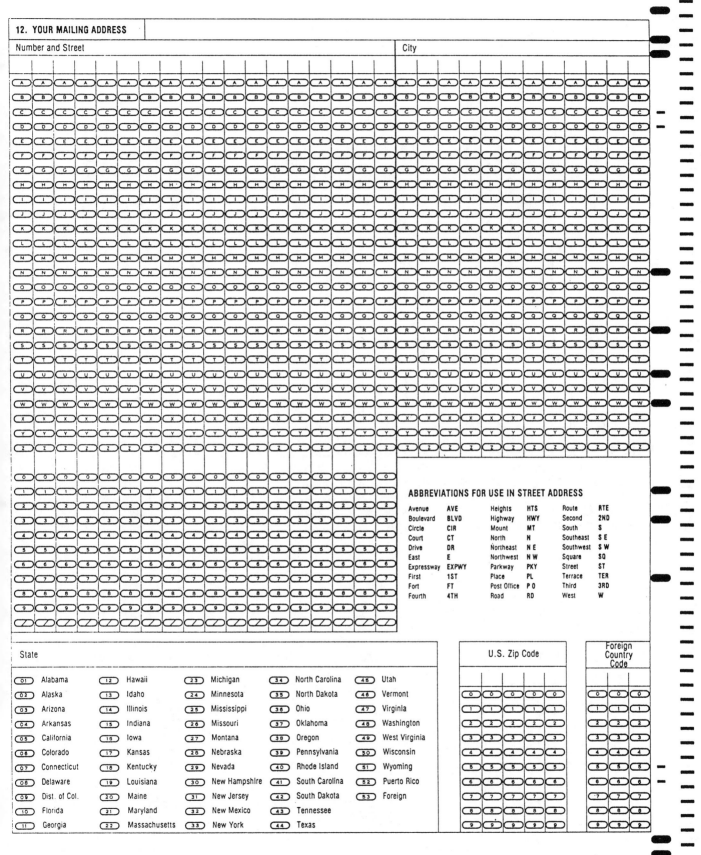

ABBREVIATIONS FOR USE IN STREET ADDRESS

Avenue	AVE	Heights	HTS	Route	RTE
Boulevard	BLVD	Highway	HWY	Second	2ND
Circle	CIR	Mount	MT	South	S
Court	CT	North	N	Southeast	S E
Drive	DR	Northeast	N E	Southwest	S W
East	E	Northwest	N W	Square	SQ
Expressway	EXPWY	Parkway	PKY	Street	ST
First	1ST	Place	PL	Terrace	TER
Fort	FT	Post Office	P O	Third	3RD
Fourth	4TH	Road	RD	West	W

State

01 Alabama	12 Hawaii	23 Michigan	34 North Carolina	45 Utah
02 Alaska	13 Idaho	24 Minnesota	35 North Dakota	46 Vermont
03 Arizona	14 Illinois	25 Mississippi	36 Ohio	47 Virginia
04 Arkansas	15 Indiana	26 Missouri	37 Oklahoma	48 Washington
05 California	16 Iowa	27 Montana	38 Oregon	49 West Virginia
06 Colorado	17 Kansas	28 Nebraska	39 Pennsylvania	50 Wisconsin
07 Connecticut	18 Kentucky	29 Nevada	40 Rhode Island	51 Wyoming
08 Delaware	19 Louisiana	30 New Hampshire	41 South Carolina	52 Puerto Rico
09 Dist. of Col.	20 Maine	31 New Jersey	42 South Dakota	53 Foreign
10 Florida	21 Maryland	32 New Mexico	43 Tennessee	
11 Georgia	22 Massachusetts	33 New York	44 Texas	

U.S. Zip Code

Foreign Country Code

EXAMINATION #1

Your Name (Print): _____
Last   First   M.I

A. Print

Examination Name: _____ **Form Designation:** _____

B. TEST CODE

0	0	0	0	0
1	1	1	1	1
2	2	2	2	2
3	3	3	3	3
4	4	4	4	4
5	5	5	5	5
6	6	6	6	6
7	7	7	7	7
8	8	8	8	8
9	9	9	9	9

C. Are you going to take the optional essay portion of this examination?

1   Yes

2   No

D. TEST BOOK SERIAL NUMBER

0	0	0	0	0	0
1	1	1	1	1	1
2	2	2	2	2	2
3	3	3	3	3	3
4	4	4	4	4	4
5	5	5	5	5	5
6	6	6	6	6	6
7	7	7	7	7	7
8	8	8	8	8	8
9	9	9	9	9	9

Be sure each mark is dark and completely fills the intended oval. If you erase, do so completely. You may find more answer responses than you need for one complete 90-minute examination. If so, please leave the extra ovals blank.

1 A B C D E   31 A B C D E   61 A B C D E   91 A B C D E   121 A B C D E
2 A B C D E   32 A B C D E   62 A B C D E   92 A B C D E   122 A B C D E
3 A B C D E   33 A B C D E   63 A B C D E   93 A B C D E   123 A B C D E
4 A B C D E   34 A B C D E   64 A B C D E   94 A B C D E   124 A B C D E
5 A B C D E   35 A B C D E   65 A B C D E   95 A B C D E   125 A B C D E
6 A B C D E   36 A B C D E   66 A B C D E   96 A B C D E   126 A B C D E
7 A B C D E   37 A B C D E   67 A B C D E   97 A B C D E   127 A B C D E
8 A B C D E   38 A B C D E   68 A B C D E   98 A B C D E   128 A B C D E
9 A B C D E   39 A B C D E   69 A B C D E   99 A B C D E   129 A B C D E
10 A B C D E   40 A B C D E   70 A B C D E   100 A B C D E   130 A B C D E
11 A B C D E   41 A B C D E   71 A B C D E   101 A B C D E   131 A B C D E
12 A B C D E   42 A B C D E   72 A B C D E   102 A B C D E   132 A B C D E
13 A B C D E   43 A B C D E   73 A B C D E   103 A B C D E   133 A B C D E
14 A B C D E   44 A B C D E   74 A B C D E   104 A B C D E   134 A B C D E
15 A B C D E   45 A B C D E   75 A B C D E   105 A B C D E   135 A B C D E
16 A B C D E   46 A B C D E   76 A B C D E   106 A B C D E   136 A B C D E
17 A B C D E   47 A B C D E   77 A B C D E   107 A B C D E   137 A B C D E
18 A B C D E   48 A B C D E   78 A B C D E   108 A B C D E   138 A B C D E
19 A B C D E   49 A B C D E   79 A B C D E   109 A B C D E   139 A B C D E
20 A B C D E   50 A B C D E   80 A B C D E   110 A B C D E   140 A B C D E
21 A B C D E   51 A B C D E   81 A B C D E   111 A B C D E   141 A B C D E
22 A B C D E   52 A B C D E   82 A B C D E   112 A B C D E   142 A B C D E
23 A B C D E   53 A B C D E   83 A B C D E   113 A B C D E   143 A B C D E
24 A B C D E   54 A B C D E   84 A B C D E   114 A B C D E   144 A B C D E
25 A B C D E   55 A B C D E   85 A B C D E   115 A B C D E   145 A B C D E
26 A B C D E   56 A B C D E   86 A B C D E   116 A B C D E   146 A B C D E
27 A B C D E   57 A B C D E   87 A B C D E   117 A B C D E   147 A B C D E
28 A B C D E   58 A B C D E   88 A B C D E   118 A B C D E   148 A B C D E
29 A B C D E   59 A B C D E   89 A B C D E   119 A B C D E   149 A B C D E
30 A B C D E   60 A B C D E   90 A B C D E   120 A B C D E   150 A B C D E

DO NOT WRITE IN THESE BOXES.

1R	1W	10	2R	2W	20	3R	3W	30	4R	4W	40	5R	5W	50	6R	6W	60	7R	7W	70	8R	8W	80
9R	9W	90	10R	10W	100	11R	11W	110	12R	12W	120	13R	13W	130	14R	14W	140	15R	15W	150	16R	16W	160

EXAMINATION #2

A. Print

Examination Name: _____ Form Designation: _____

B. TEST CODE

⓪	⓪	⓪	⓪	⓪
①	①	①	①	①
②	②	②	②	②
③	③	③	③	③
④	④	④	④	④
⑤	⑤	⑤	⑤	⑤
⑥	⑥	⑥	⑥	⑥
⑦	⑦	⑦	⑦	⑦
⑧	⑧	⑧	⑧	⑧
⑨	⑨	⑨	⑨	⑨

C. Are you going to take the optional essay portion of this examination?

① Yes

② No

D. TEST BOOK SERIAL NUMBER

⓪	⓪	⓪	⓪	⓪	⓪
①	①	①	①	①	①
②	②	②	②	②	②
③	③	③	③	③	③
④	④	④	④	④	④
⑤	⑤	⑤	⑤	⑤	⑤
⑥	⑥	⑥	⑥	⑥	⑥
⑦	⑦	⑦	⑦	⑦	⑦
⑧	⑧	⑧	⑧	⑧	⑧
⑨	⑨	⑨	⑨	⑨	⑨

Be sure each mark is dark and completely fills the intended oval. If you erase, do so completely. You may find more answer responses than you need for one complete 90-minute examination. If so, please leave the extra ovals blank.

1 Ⓐ Ⓑ Ⓒ Ⓓ Ⓔ   31 Ⓐ Ⓑ Ⓒ Ⓓ Ⓔ   61 Ⓐ Ⓑ Ⓒ Ⓓ Ⓔ   91 Ⓐ Ⓑ Ⓒ Ⓓ Ⓔ   121 Ⓐ Ⓑ Ⓒ Ⓓ Ⓔ
2 Ⓐ Ⓑ Ⓒ Ⓓ Ⓔ   32 Ⓐ Ⓑ Ⓒ Ⓓ Ⓔ   62 Ⓐ Ⓑ Ⓒ Ⓓ Ⓔ   92 Ⓐ Ⓑ Ⓒ Ⓓ Ⓔ   122 Ⓐ Ⓑ Ⓒ Ⓓ Ⓔ
3 Ⓐ Ⓑ Ⓒ Ⓓ Ⓔ   33 Ⓐ Ⓑ Ⓒ Ⓓ Ⓔ   63 Ⓐ Ⓑ Ⓒ Ⓓ Ⓔ   93 Ⓐ Ⓑ Ⓒ Ⓓ Ⓔ   123 Ⓐ Ⓑ Ⓒ Ⓓ Ⓔ
4 Ⓐ Ⓑ Ⓒ Ⓓ Ⓔ   34 Ⓐ Ⓑ Ⓒ Ⓓ Ⓔ   64 Ⓐ Ⓑ Ⓒ Ⓓ Ⓔ   94 Ⓐ Ⓑ Ⓒ Ⓓ Ⓔ   124 Ⓐ Ⓑ Ⓒ Ⓓ Ⓔ
5 Ⓐ Ⓑ Ⓒ Ⓓ Ⓔ   35 Ⓐ Ⓑ Ⓒ Ⓓ Ⓔ   65 Ⓐ Ⓑ Ⓒ Ⓓ Ⓔ   95 Ⓐ Ⓑ Ⓒ Ⓓ Ⓔ   125 Ⓐ Ⓑ Ⓒ Ⓓ Ⓔ
6 Ⓐ Ⓑ Ⓒ Ⓓ Ⓔ   36 Ⓐ Ⓑ Ⓒ Ⓓ Ⓔ   66 Ⓐ Ⓑ Ⓒ Ⓓ Ⓔ   96 Ⓐ Ⓑ Ⓒ Ⓓ Ⓔ   126 Ⓐ Ⓑ Ⓒ Ⓓ Ⓔ
7 Ⓐ Ⓑ Ⓒ Ⓓ Ⓔ   37 Ⓐ Ⓑ Ⓒ Ⓓ Ⓔ   67 Ⓐ Ⓑ Ⓒ Ⓓ Ⓔ   97 Ⓐ Ⓑ Ⓒ Ⓓ Ⓔ   127 Ⓐ Ⓑ Ⓒ Ⓓ Ⓔ
8 Ⓐ Ⓑ Ⓒ Ⓓ Ⓔ   38 Ⓐ Ⓑ Ⓒ Ⓓ Ⓔ   68 Ⓐ Ⓑ Ⓒ Ⓓ Ⓔ   98 Ⓐ Ⓑ Ⓒ Ⓓ Ⓔ   128 Ⓐ Ⓑ Ⓒ Ⓓ Ⓔ
9 Ⓐ Ⓑ Ⓒ Ⓓ Ⓔ   39 Ⓐ Ⓑ Ⓒ Ⓓ Ⓔ   69 Ⓐ Ⓑ Ⓒ Ⓓ Ⓔ   99 Ⓐ Ⓑ Ⓒ Ⓓ Ⓔ   129 Ⓐ Ⓑ Ⓒ Ⓓ Ⓔ
10 Ⓐ Ⓑ Ⓒ Ⓓ Ⓔ   40 Ⓐ Ⓑ Ⓒ Ⓓ Ⓔ   70 Ⓐ Ⓑ Ⓒ Ⓓ Ⓔ   100 Ⓐ Ⓑ Ⓒ Ⓓ Ⓔ   130 Ⓐ Ⓑ Ⓒ Ⓓ Ⓔ
11 Ⓐ Ⓑ Ⓒ Ⓓ Ⓔ   41 Ⓐ Ⓑ Ⓒ Ⓓ Ⓔ   71 Ⓐ Ⓑ Ⓒ Ⓓ Ⓔ   101 Ⓐ Ⓑ Ⓒ Ⓓ Ⓔ   131 Ⓐ Ⓑ Ⓒ Ⓓ Ⓔ
12 Ⓐ Ⓑ Ⓒ Ⓓ Ⓔ   42 Ⓐ Ⓑ Ⓒ Ⓓ Ⓔ   72 Ⓐ Ⓑ Ⓒ Ⓓ Ⓔ   102 Ⓐ Ⓑ Ⓒ Ⓓ Ⓔ   132 Ⓐ Ⓑ Ⓒ Ⓓ Ⓔ
13 Ⓐ Ⓑ Ⓒ Ⓓ Ⓔ   43 Ⓐ Ⓑ Ⓒ Ⓓ Ⓔ   73 Ⓐ Ⓑ Ⓒ Ⓓ Ⓔ   103 Ⓐ Ⓑ Ⓒ Ⓓ Ⓔ   133 Ⓐ Ⓑ Ⓒ Ⓓ Ⓔ
14 Ⓐ Ⓑ Ⓒ Ⓓ Ⓔ   44 Ⓐ Ⓑ Ⓒ Ⓓ Ⓔ   74 Ⓐ Ⓑ Ⓒ Ⓓ Ⓔ   104 Ⓐ Ⓑ Ⓒ Ⓓ Ⓔ   134 Ⓐ Ⓑ Ⓒ Ⓓ Ⓔ
15 Ⓐ Ⓑ Ⓒ Ⓓ Ⓔ   45 Ⓐ Ⓑ Ⓒ Ⓓ Ⓔ   75 Ⓐ Ⓑ Ⓒ Ⓓ Ⓔ   105 Ⓐ Ⓑ Ⓒ Ⓓ Ⓔ   135 Ⓐ Ⓑ Ⓒ Ⓓ Ⓔ
16 Ⓐ Ⓑ Ⓒ Ⓓ Ⓔ   46 Ⓐ Ⓑ Ⓒ Ⓓ Ⓔ   76 Ⓐ Ⓑ Ⓒ Ⓓ Ⓔ   106 Ⓐ Ⓑ Ⓒ Ⓓ Ⓔ   136 Ⓐ Ⓑ Ⓒ Ⓓ Ⓔ
17 Ⓐ Ⓑ Ⓒ Ⓓ Ⓔ   47 Ⓐ Ⓑ Ⓒ Ⓓ Ⓔ   77 Ⓐ Ⓑ Ⓒ Ⓓ Ⓔ   107 Ⓐ Ⓑ Ⓒ Ⓓ Ⓔ   137 Ⓐ Ⓑ Ⓒ Ⓓ Ⓔ
18 Ⓐ Ⓑ Ⓒ Ⓓ Ⓔ   48 Ⓐ Ⓑ Ⓒ Ⓓ Ⓔ   78 Ⓐ Ⓑ Ⓒ Ⓓ Ⓔ   108 Ⓐ Ⓑ Ⓒ Ⓓ Ⓔ   138 Ⓐ Ⓑ Ⓒ Ⓓ Ⓔ
19 Ⓐ Ⓑ Ⓒ Ⓓ Ⓔ   49 Ⓐ Ⓑ Ⓒ Ⓓ Ⓔ   79 Ⓐ Ⓑ Ⓒ Ⓓ Ⓔ   109 Ⓐ Ⓑ Ⓒ Ⓓ Ⓔ   139 Ⓐ Ⓑ Ⓒ Ⓓ Ⓔ
20 Ⓐ Ⓑ Ⓒ Ⓓ Ⓔ   50 Ⓐ Ⓑ Ⓒ Ⓓ Ⓔ   80 Ⓐ Ⓑ Ⓒ Ⓓ Ⓔ   110 Ⓐ Ⓑ Ⓒ Ⓓ Ⓔ   140 Ⓐ Ⓑ Ⓒ Ⓓ Ⓔ
21 Ⓐ Ⓑ Ⓒ Ⓓ Ⓔ   51 Ⓐ Ⓑ Ⓒ Ⓓ Ⓔ   81 Ⓐ Ⓑ Ⓒ Ⓓ Ⓔ   111 Ⓐ Ⓑ Ⓒ Ⓓ Ⓔ   141 Ⓐ Ⓑ Ⓒ Ⓓ Ⓔ
22 Ⓐ Ⓑ Ⓒ Ⓓ Ⓔ   52 Ⓐ Ⓑ Ⓒ Ⓓ Ⓔ   82 Ⓐ Ⓑ Ⓒ Ⓓ Ⓔ   112 Ⓐ Ⓑ Ⓒ Ⓓ Ⓔ   142 Ⓐ Ⓑ Ⓒ Ⓓ Ⓔ
23 Ⓐ Ⓑ Ⓒ Ⓓ Ⓔ   53 Ⓐ Ⓑ Ⓒ Ⓓ Ⓔ   83 Ⓐ Ⓑ Ⓒ Ⓓ Ⓔ   113 Ⓐ Ⓑ Ⓒ Ⓓ Ⓔ   143 Ⓐ Ⓑ Ⓒ Ⓓ Ⓔ
24 Ⓐ Ⓑ Ⓒ Ⓓ Ⓔ   54 Ⓐ Ⓑ Ⓒ Ⓓ Ⓔ   84 Ⓐ Ⓑ Ⓒ Ⓓ Ⓔ   114 Ⓐ Ⓑ Ⓒ Ⓓ Ⓔ   144 Ⓐ Ⓑ Ⓒ Ⓓ Ⓔ
25 Ⓐ Ⓑ Ⓒ Ⓓ Ⓔ   55 Ⓐ Ⓑ Ⓒ Ⓓ Ⓔ   85 Ⓐ Ⓑ Ⓒ Ⓓ Ⓔ   115 Ⓐ Ⓑ Ⓒ Ⓓ Ⓔ   145 Ⓐ Ⓑ Ⓒ Ⓓ Ⓔ
26 Ⓐ Ⓑ Ⓒ Ⓓ Ⓔ   56 Ⓐ Ⓑ Ⓒ Ⓓ Ⓔ   86 Ⓐ Ⓑ Ⓒ Ⓓ Ⓔ   116 Ⓐ Ⓑ Ⓒ Ⓓ Ⓔ   146 Ⓐ Ⓑ Ⓒ Ⓓ Ⓔ
27 Ⓐ Ⓑ Ⓒ Ⓓ Ⓔ   57 Ⓐ Ⓑ Ⓒ Ⓓ Ⓔ   87 Ⓐ Ⓑ Ⓒ Ⓓ Ⓔ   117 Ⓐ Ⓑ Ⓒ Ⓓ Ⓔ   147 Ⓐ Ⓑ Ⓒ Ⓓ Ⓔ
28 Ⓐ Ⓑ Ⓒ Ⓓ Ⓔ   58 Ⓐ Ⓑ Ⓒ Ⓓ Ⓔ   88 Ⓐ Ⓑ Ⓒ Ⓓ Ⓔ   118 Ⓐ Ⓑ Ⓒ Ⓓ Ⓔ   148 Ⓐ Ⓑ Ⓒ Ⓓ Ⓔ
29 Ⓐ Ⓑ Ⓒ Ⓓ Ⓔ   59 Ⓐ Ⓑ Ⓒ Ⓓ Ⓔ   89 Ⓐ Ⓑ Ⓒ Ⓓ Ⓔ   119 Ⓐ Ⓑ Ⓒ Ⓓ Ⓔ   149 Ⓐ Ⓑ Ⓒ Ⓓ Ⓔ
30 Ⓐ Ⓑ Ⓒ Ⓓ Ⓔ   60 Ⓐ Ⓑ Ⓒ Ⓓ Ⓔ   90 Ⓐ Ⓑ Ⓒ Ⓓ Ⓔ   120 Ⓐ Ⓑ Ⓒ Ⓓ Ⓔ   150 Ⓐ Ⓑ Ⓒ Ⓓ Ⓔ

DO NOT WRITE IN THESE BOXES.

1R	1W	10	2R	2W	20	3R	3W	30	4R	4W	40	5R	5W	50	6R	6W	60	7R	7W	70	8R	8W	80

9R	9W	90	10R	10W	100	11R	11W	110	12R	12W	120	13R	13W	130	14R	14W	140	15R	15W	150	16R	16W	160

Short Sample Test

CLEP INTRODUCTION TO MANAGEMENT

Time: 25 minutes   25 questions

DIRECTIONS: Each of the following questions contain incomplete statements followed by five suggested answers or completions. Select the one that is best in each case.

1.   Management is defined as being a:

(A) policy
(B) principle
(C) procedure
(D) process
(E) problem

2.   The management function that initiates action to carry out plans and achieve goals is:

(A) planning
(B) organizing
(C) staffing
(D) directing
(E) controlling

3.   The Hawthorne Studies mark the start of:

(A) the behavioral or human relations approach to management
(B) scientific management
(C) classical management
(D) the systems approach
(E) contingency approach

4.   "Stakeholders" include:

(A) those who are affected by what the organization does
(B) the organization's owners (e.g., stockholders)
(C) the organization's management
(D) members of the community
(E) all of the above

5.   Skills which appear to be most important to the highest levels of management are _____ skills:

(A) accounting
(B) computational
(C) conceptual
(D) financial
(E) technical

6. Which ONE of the following is NOT a "single-use plan"?

(A) procedure
(B) program
(C) project
(D) budget
(E) none of the above (all are single-use plans)

7. A plan for the use of resources and expected results stated in quantitative terms is called a:

(A) forecast
(B) developmental device
(C) cost control
(D) budget
(E) resource reference list

8. Problem solving involves:

(A) thinking
(B) finding or developing alternatives
(C) forecasting
(D) staff
(E) all of the above could be true

9. In contrast to the "rational economic man" of the economic theorist Herbert Simon, the real-world "administrative man":

(A) has "complete information" and "optimizes"
(B) operates in a probability condition of "certainty"
(C) has "bounded rationality" and "satisfices"
(D) bases decisions on careful analysis of probability matrices
(E) none of the above

10. Under decentralization decision-making is pushed to the:

(A) Board of Directors
(B) lower levels of the organization
(C) staff
(D) stakeholders
(E) none of the above

11. An organization chart shows all of the following except:

(A) qualifications of employees
(B) division of work
(C) line or staff roles
(D) authority relationships
(E) all of the above are shown (there are no exceptions)

12. According to the "strategy and structure" hypothesis of A.D. Chandler, for companies pursuing a single-business strategy, the most appropriate organizational form is (a):

(A) functional structure
(B) multi-national firm (MNF)
(C) matrix
(D) product-division structure
(E) none of the above

13. A term that means just the opposite of "organic" is:

(A) participative
(B) urban
(C) democratic
(D) ad hoc
(E) mechanistic

14. The process of developing complete information about what a job involves and what skills are needed to do it is called:

(A) job description
(B) job evaluation
(C) job matriculation
(D) job analysis
(E) none of the above

15. A department of wage and salary administration would ordinarily:

(A) be found in the Personnel or Human Resources Department
(B) be concerned with compensation management
(C) be under the direct supervision of the chief financial officer
(D) be part of Research and Development
(E) both A and B

16. The organization most likely to be involved in an attempt by a union to organize the employees of a company is:

(A) NLRB
(B) NFL
(C) NRA
(D) NTSB
(E) none of the above would be involved

17. Which of the following is a source of bias or error in judgments of job applicants made by employment interviewers:

(A) stereotyping
(B) standardization
(C) role-overload
(D) Type A personality
(E) Type B personality

18. Something that follows behavior and causes an increase in the probability of its reoccurrence is called a:

(A) distractor
(B) punishment
(C) reinforcer
(D) transactional event
(E) none of the above

19. In the Ohio State University Studies, a supervisor who shows concern for subordinates and listens to their problems and ideas is said to show the behavior of:

(A) consideration
(B) consultation
(C) initiation of structure
(D) projection
(E) none of the above

20. The _____ approach holds that the leaders possess certain personal characteristics that set them apart from followers—such as intelligence, energy, aggressiveness.

(A) leader set-aside
(B) behavioral
(C) dimensional
(D) trait
(E) follower differential

21. When Joe's boss expects him to push his men hard for higher production while Joe's subordinates think he should be reasonable and take it easy on them, we have an example of:

(A) role overload
(B) production-centered leadership
(C) leadership in crisis
(D) visioning skills
(E) role conflict

22. Terms associated in some way with inventory control include all of the following EXCEPT:

(A) PERT
(B) MRP I
(C) EOQ
(D) PIPC
(E) none of the above

23. PERT stands for:

(A) Production Essential Required for Termination
(B) Program Evaluation Review Technique
(C) Programmers Equitable Retirement Trust
(D) Prerequisites for Efficiency, Reinforcement and Training
(E) Polyethylene Register Technology

24. Financial ratios in common use for evaluating the financial condition of the enterprise include all but one of the following. Which is NOT a financial ratio?

    (A) break-even point
    (B) current ratio (current assets/current liabilities)
    (C) acid-test ratio (cash and receivables/current liabilities)
    (D) inventory turnover (cost of goods sold/average annual inventory)
    (E) assets turnover (sales/total assets)

25. Included in the hardware of a computer system would be which of the following elements?

    (A) central processing unit
    (B) input unit(s)
    (C) storage unit(s)
    (D) all of the above
    (E) none of the above

Answers To Short Sample Test

1. D   Management is a process. A, B, and C are types of plans.

2. D   The Directing (or Leading) function involves implementing plans—thus, taking action.

3. A   The Hawthorne experiments conducted by Roethlisberger and Mayo led to the Human Relations Movement which viewed the factory as a social system in which social-psychological factors were thought to be as important (or more important) for productivity as the physical factors which had been emphasized by Scientific Management.

4. E   All of the above: stakeholders are those who can affect the enterprise and are affected by it.

5. C   Conceptual skills increase in importance as we move up the organizational hierarchy. Purely technical skills predominate at lower levels. Some have argued that interpersonal skills are important at all levels, lower, middle and top.

6. A   A procedure is a standing plan. The others (B,C,D) are single-use plans.

7. D   Budgets are quantitative statements of authorized resources and expected results.

8. B   The preferred answer is "finding or developing alternatives" (solutions). In a broad sense, of course, E (all of the above) could also be correct.

9. C   Simon's "administrative man", operating with "bounded rationality", settles for the solution that satisfies his criteria and does not demand the best possible solution.

10. B   Decentralization moves authority away from the top of the organization to lower and outer levels.

11. A   Qualifications (e.g., experience, education, ability, motivation) of position holders are NOT shown on an organization chart.

12. A   A functional (and centralized) structure is most appropriate.

13. E   Mechanistic structures can be equated roughly to the machine bureaucracy. In contrast, organic structures tend to be more informal, less rigid, more open to change, more able to shift responsibility and authority in response to change, less centralized and less authoritarian.

14. D   Job analysis is the complete process.

    Job description is part of the process and explains the duties and function of the job.

    Job evaluation determines the pay for the job.

15. E Both A and B. "Wage and salary administration" and "compensation management" mean the same thing. They are handled in the Human Resources Department.

16. A NLRB—initials for the National Labor Relations Board, established under the National Labor Relations Act (NLRA—the Wagner Act). One of its responsibilities is to supervise union organizing elections and, if the employees vote in favor of union representation, to certify the union as the official representative or agent of the employee bargaining unit.

17. A Stereotyping—a common error in interviewer and rater judgments—is the evaluation of a person on the basis of membership in a group or category (e.g., farmers, women, blacks, etc.) rather than on the basis of the individual's actual performance or abilities.

18. C A reinforcer or reinforcement is anything that strengthens the behavior that it follows (or makes it more likely to be repeated).

19. A Consideration. The other category of leader behavior from the Ohio State studies was "initiating structure."

20. D The trait approach claims that the possession of certain personal attributes is what makes leaders different from followers.

21. E This is an example of role conflict, actually of "intra-role" conflict which means conflict within (intra) the same role. The supervisor role is typical in that the boss has different role expectations than do those supervised.

22. A PERT is NOT concerned with inventory control.

23. B PERT are the initials of Program Evaluation Review Technique—a method for planning, analyzing and controlling program schedules.

24. A Break-even point is NOT a financial ratio. See text for definitions of B, C, D and E.

25. D A computer system's hardware components include central processing, input, output and storage units.

Sample Test

CLEP INTRODUCTION TO MANAGEMENT

SECTION I

Time: 45 minutes   50 questions

DIRECTIONS: Each of the following questions contain incomplete statements followed by five suggested answers or completions. Select the one that is best in each case.

1. The management function that focuses on the FUTURE is:

   (A) planning
   (B) organizing
   (C) staffing
   (D) directing
   (E) controlling

2. The management function that deals with the structuring of authority relationships is:

   (A) planning
   (B) organizing
   (C) staffing
   (D) directing
   (E) controlling

3. The management function that has to do with finding people to fill the positions in the organization is:

   (A) planning
   (B) organizing
   (C) staffing
   (D) directing
   (E) controlling

4. The management function that makes sure that things go as planned is:

   (A) planning
   (B) organizing
   (C) staffing
   (D) directing
   (E) controlling

5. Which of the following is an example of middle management:

   (A) President
   (B) Foreman
   (C) Plant Manager
   (D) Crew Chief
   (E) none of the above

6. Which of the following is NOT a category of managerial roles discussed by Mintzberg:

   (A) interpersonal
   (B) prudential
   (C) informational
   (D) decisional
   (E) There are no exceptions. All are managerial role categories according to Mintzberg.

7. People associated with Scientific Management would include:

   (A) Fayol, Urwick
   (B) Taylor, Gilbreth
   (C) Roethlisberger, Mayo
   (D) Barnard, Simon
   (E) Drucker

8. Classical Management Theory would be associated with:

   (A) Henri Fayol
   (B) Henry Ford
   (C) Peter Drucker
   (D) Herbert Simon
   (E) Sigmund Freud

9. The idea that there is NO one best way of managing which applies to all situations—that the approach needs to be tailored to the situation at hand—is called:

   (A) classical management
   (B) scientific management
   (C) behavioral approach
   (D) contingency approach
   (E) best approach

10. The view that the various parts of an organization affect one another and that the organization is affected by the external environment and in turn affects the environment illustrates:

    (A) the classical approach
    (B) behavioral approach
    (C) contingency approach
    (D) systems approach
    (E) scientific management

11. The environment of organizations includes:

    (A) governments
    (B) laws
    (C) customers
    (D) other organizations
    (E) all of the above (and more)

12. The ethical dimension of business decisions requires that the decision maker consider:

    (A) what is feasible
    (B) what is profitable
    (C) what is socially acceptable
    (D) all of the above
    (E) none of the above

13. One of the following is NOT a form of international business activity:

    (A) direct investment
    (B) portfolio investment
    (C) mediation and arbitration
    (D) joint venture
    (E) multi-national firm

14. A business corporation with world headquarters in its home country and with semi-autonomous subsidiary companies or businesses in many other countries is frequently called a:

    (A) Multiple Equity Corporation (MEC)
    (B) Multilateral Business (MLB)
    (C) Multiple Personality Corporation (MPC)
    (D) Multi-national firm (MNF)
    (E) Parabolic Corporation

15. A company that sells a similar product worldwide (perhaps with marketing subsidiaries in different countries) is a(an):

    (A) gigantic corporation
    (B) international corporation
    (C) global corporation
    (D) interstate corporation
    (E) none of the above

16. The steps in the planning process include:

    (A) person; situation; position
    (B) identify goals; develop alternatives; choose best course; develop objectives and responsibilities; review
    (C) measure performance; communicate deviations to those responsible; follow up
    (D) determine needed solution; assign responsibilities; monitor results
    (E) organize; staff; direct; lead; control

17. Strategic plans and broad organizational policies would usually be the responsibility of:

    (A) management consultants
    (B) the federal government
    (C) top management
    (D) first-line management
    (E) project manager

18. In the hierarchy of plans, strategies would be developed before:

    (A) mission statements
    (B) operational plans
    (C) organizational goals
    (D) all of the above
    (E) none of the above

19. Standing plans include which ONE of the following:

    (A) budgets
    (B) projects
    (C) forecasts
    (D) policies
    (E) none of the above

20. _____ are guides to thinking and decision-making:

    (A) actions
    (B) controls
    (C) opinions
    (D) policies
    (E) rules

21. If a ten-year strategic plan is revised each year, always projecting ten years into the future, this would be an example of:

    (A) limited action planning
    (B) a rolling plan
    (C) reverse-sequence planning
    (D) the folly of planning
    (E) an operating plan

22. Peter Drucker's "Key Result Areas" include all but one of the following:

    (A) control
    (B) innovation
    (C) productivity
    (D) social responsibilities
    (E) none of the above (all are key result areas of Drucker)

23. All plans are also:

    (A) budgets
    (B) control tools
    (C) forecasts
    (D) generalizations
    (E) rationalizations

24. Interpreted broadly, the term "sales forecast" refers to the predicted or expected future demand for the organization's products or services. An example would be:

(A) predicted enrollment next year at a university
(B) the number of jellybeans sold last year in Peoria, Illinois
(C) the number of machinists currently assigned to the Ajax Project
(D) the possibility that nuclear fusion will be the primary energy source twenty years from now
(E) none of the above

25. Methods of forecasting sales include which one of the following:

(A) asking the opinion of experienced marketing executives
(B) asking consumers about their purchasing plans and preferences
(C) assuming that next year will be about the same as this year
(D) all of the above
(E) none of the above

26. According to Nobel laureate Herbert Simon, decision-making involves three phases which are:

(A) input; transformation; output
(B) program; project; procedure
(C) intelligence; design; choice
(D) argument; synopsis; praxis
(E) planning; directing; controlling

27. Most authorities agree that it is important at the outset of the problem-solving process or before starting the decision-making process, to:

(A) define the problem
(B) select a course of action
(C) develop contingency plans
(D) vote on the options
(E) all of the above

28. The terms "states of nature", "contingent value", "probability", and "expected value" would be best associated with a(an):

(A) EOQ chart
(B) break-even chart
(C) PERT chart
(D) payoff table or payoff matrix
(E) none of the above

29. All of the information shown in a payoff matrix can also be (and often is) shown by a:

(A) density function
(B) transparency analog
(C) algebraic inversion layer
(D) decision tree
(E) none of the above

30. In a break-even chart, the vertical axis shows:

    (A) dollars
    (B) quantity sold
    (C) per capita income
    (D) total revenues
    (E) net income

31. In a break-even chart, the break-even point is that point where:

    (A) total costs equal total revenues
    (B) you are making a profit
    (C) fixed costs plus variable costs equal total costs
    (D) all of the above
    (E) none of the above

32. There is a limit to the number of subordinates a single person can supervise. This is the principle of:

    (A) unity of command
    (B) chain of command
    (C) the exception
    (D) span of control
    (E) none of the above

33. According to the _____ principle, once policies and procedures have been established, most things should be handled at lower organizational levels and only unusual matters should be referred to higher levels for decision. What is the principle?

    (A) unity of command
    (B) chain of command
    (C) departmentation
    (D) span of control
    (E) none of the above

34. The scalar principle states that there should be:

    (A) only one superior for each subordinate
    (B) equality in the scales of justice
    (C) a place and time for everything
    (D) a clear chain of command from top to bottom
    (E) none of the above

35. When the Vice President for Human Resources issues instructions on personnel reporting procedures to the Personnel Staff Specialist assigned to the Plant Manager, this would be an example of the use of:

    (A) accountability authority
    (B) bases of departmentation
    (C) functional authority
    (D) line authority
    (E) informal authority

36. Bureaucracy, as described by Max Weber, had all but one of the following characteristics:

    (A) organization structure is hierarchical
    (B) activities to achieve goals are assigned as fixed official duties
    (C) decisions are governed by a system of abstract rules and regulations
    (D) officials are selected from the aristocracy or on the basis of family power and status
    (E) employees have a career orientation; they are professionals with lifetime tenure

37. Joan Woodward classified production technologies into three types, one of which is listed below:

    (A) unit and small batch
    (B) manual labor
    (C) computerized
    (D) high tech
    (E) none of the above

38. Rensis Likert's "System 4" theory proposed that organizations should be:

    (A) based on strict one-on-one authority relationships
    (B) rationally designed to support social goals
    (C) systems of overlapping groups
    (D) free-standing entrepreneurial structures
    (E) none of the above

39. According to classical management theory, authority and responsibility should be:

    (A) separated
    (B) vertical
    (C) horizontal
    (D) equal
    (E) none of the above

40. Peachy Computers has four Vice Presidents (VP) reporting to the CEO: VP for Research and Development, VP for Engineering and Manufacturing, VP for Marketing, VP for Finance and Controller. What kind of departmentalization is involved here?

    (A) product
    (B) territorial
    (C) customer
    (D) functional
    (E) none of the above

41. A principle of organization that says that each subordinate should report to only one superior is called the principle of:

    (A) unity of force
    (B) unity of command
    (C) unity of direction
    (D) unity of reporting
    (E) none of the above

42. If the Sales Manager has the authority to hire, fire and give direction to salesmen, this is what kind of relationship?

 (A) a line relationship
 (B) an efficient relationship
 (C) a staff relationship
 (D) an ambiguous relationship
 (E) none of the above

43. According to Alfred D. Chandler in Strategy and Structure, a diversified growth strategy in a large enterprise should lead to an organizational structure that is:

 (A) monopolistic
 (B) under government control or ownership
 (C) divisionalized by product and decentralized
 (D) of a matrix form
 (E) centralized and functionally departmented

44. In the Classical Management Theories method of management and in Max Weber's theory of bureaucracy, it was assumed that in a hierarchical organization, knowledge and experience were greatest:

 (A) at the point where the problem existed
 (B) at the top of the organization
 (C) at the middle management levels
 (D) at the bottom of the structure
 (E) among the organization's stakeholders

45. The extent to which an organization operates on the basis of written rules, procedures and other documents is called:

 (A) action-orientation
 (B) decision-congruence
 (C) formalization
 (D) span of control
 (E) technological integration

46. The term, _____, refers to the number of different kinds of jobs together with the number of levels of hierarchy in the organization.

 (A) sequential interdependence
 (B) turbulence
 (C) formalization
 (D) span of control
 (E) complexity

47. In general the higher the level of interdependence required between various parts of the organization, the greater:

 (A) the need for coordinating mechanisms
 (B) number of levels of hierarchy
 (C) the degree of decentralization possible
 (D) the dependence on the environment
 (E) the appropriateness of a functional form of structure

48. The management function that matches people with the demands of the organizational structure is called:

   (A) planning
   (B) programming
   (C) staffing
   (D) structuring
   (E) none of the above

49. The Human Resources or Personnel Manager would most likely have staff or functional authority for organizational compliance with:

   (A) Clean Air Act of 1970
   (B) EEO Laws
   (C) State Fish and Game Regulations
   (D) Food and Drug Administration Rulings
   (E) none of the above

50. Title VII of the Civil Rights Act of 1964 bars discrimination in employment based on:

   (A) race, color or religion
   (B) sex or national origin
   (C) height and weight
   (D) A and B but not C
   (E) none of the above

STOP

If you finish before the time limit is reached, you may check your work on this section only.

SECTION II

DIRECTIONS: Each of the following questions contain incomplete statements followed by five suggested answers or completions. Select the one that is best in each case.

51. In a large organization, staff specialists familiar with the laws and court decisions on selection, hiring, assignment and promotion would be found in the:

    (A) Personnel or Human Resources Department
    (B) branch offices
    (C) Production Planning Department
    (D) Marketing Department
    (E) none of the above

52. The qualifications needed by someone to perform a specific job successfully would be detailed in a (the):

    (A) special job evaluation
    (B) job specialist's file
    (C) qualifications detail
    (D) job specification
    (E) none of the above

53. The process of studying jobs for the purpose of determining how much money should be paid for performing them is called:

    (A) performance appraisal
    (B) job analysis
    (C) job specification
    (D) job evaluation
    (E) none of the above

54. Information about a person's qualifications and aptitude for a job can be obtained from all of the following EXCEPT:

    (A) completed employment applications
    (B) resumes
    (C) Gantt Charts
    (D) standardized tests
    (E) there are no exceptions

55. In almost every organization the selection process includes one or more:

    (A) interviews
    (B) internships
    (C) interdepartmental committees
    (D) personality tests
    (E) all of the above

56. An important consideration in compensation management (or wage and salary administration) is that the employees of the organization view the compensation system as:

   (A) equitable
   (B) understandable
   (C) related to performance
   (D) all of the above
   (E) none of the above is important

57. Which of the following is a principal employee training method:

   (A) job evaluation
   (B) time and motion study
   (C) task structure
   (D) on-job-training (OJT)
   (E) none of the above

58. Most grievance procedures, even under union contracts, attempt to have the grievance resolved:

   (A) by compulsory arbitration
   (B) with the CEO
   (C) with the immediate supervisor
   (D) by the Personnel Department
   (E) by the AFL-CIO Executive Committee

59. Information about managerial personnel, such as age, current performance, promotability, possible replacements:

   (A) is useful for planning
   (B) is called by various names such as "replacement charts" and "manpower audit"
   (C) is useful for filling vacancies that occur without warning
   (D) all of the above
   (E) none of the above

60. Most union contracts provide as the FINAL stage of the grievance procedure:

   (A) agitation
   (B) arbitration
   (C) counseling
   (D) mediation
   (E) meditation

61. If an organization wants to select from among non-supervisory employees the best candidates for supervisor training and possible promotion to supervisory positions, the most effective and appropriate selection procedure would be:

   (A) arbitration
   (B) assessment center
   (C) job posting
   (D) job evaluation
   (E) manpower planning

62. An important first or preliminary step before planning and initiating a training program would be (a, an):

    (A) assessment centers
    (B) employee orientation program
    (C) on-the-job training (OJT)
    (D) "no-nonsense" management training
    (E) needs assessment

63. A policy of selection—and promotion-from-within—has which of the following as a drawback or disadvantage:

    (A) over-promotion to upper management levels
    (B) negative effects on employee morale
    (C) possible severe restriction on sources of new employees
    (D) lowered performance ratings
    (E) Consumer Product Safety Commission objections

64. In Maslow's Need Hierarchy model:

    (A) man has ten sets of basic needs
    (B) these needs all operate at the same time but in random and unpredictable sequence
    (C) self-fulfillment needs include hunger, thirst and sex
    (D) all of the above
    (E) none of the above

65. According to Douglas McGregor, if a manager makes the assumptions that most employees can be creative, can accept responsibility, can become capable and competent, can enjoy work—the manager:

    (A) holds to Theory X
    (B) will carefully plan, direct and control what the employee does
    (C) will make all organizational decisions unilaterally by herself
    (D) all of the above
    (E) none of the above

66. Concern for success as measured by a standard of excellence, preference for immediate concrete feedback and choice of goals of intermediate difficulty characterize persons with a high need for:

    (A) affiliation
    (B) attribution
    (C) achievement
    (D) recognition
    (E) none of the above

67. A direct practical application of the Motivator-Hygiene Theory has been:

    (A) job enrichment
    (B) piece-rate incentive systems
    (C) pay-for-performance
    (D) management by objectives
    (E) none of the above

68. When a respected supervisor thanks a subordinate for the accuracy of a report—the "thank you" is:

    (A) positive reinforcement
    (B) negative reinforcement
    (C) unnecessary
    (D) all of the above
    (E) none of the above

69. Alice Smith is a secretary. She used to bring fresh flowers to work every day but no one ever noticed; so, after a few months she stopped. This demonstrates the operant conditioning principle of:

    (A) extinction (omission of reinforcement)
    (B) positive reinforcement
    (C) negative reinforcement
    (D) punishment
    (E) none of the above

70. According to the Expectancy Model of Motivation if ANY of the elements of valence, expectancy or instrumentality:

    (A) is zero, effort or motivation will be zero
    (B) is high, effort or motivation will be zero
    (C) is the same as another, the formula will not work
    (D) all of the above
    (E) none of the above

71. The approaches to leadership which emphasize leader-follower differences in such things as intelligence, initiative, energy level and motivation are known as _____ approaches:

    (A) behavioral
    (B) classical
    (C) systems
    (D) theoretical
    (E) none of the above

72. When one induces or influences others to work toward some objective—this is one definition of:

    (A) organizing
    (B) controlling
    (C) leadership
    (D) productivity
    (E) none of the above

73. Leadership theories that assert that the same leadership style may be effective in some situations but ineffective in others are known as:

    (A) behavioral theories
    (B) contingency theories
    (C) deterministic theories
    (D) equity theories
    (E) none of the above

74. A leader who consults with subordinates and gets their suggestions when making a decision would be using a _____ type or style of leadership:

(A) superficial
(B) directive
(C) participative
(D) achievement-oriented
(E) none of the above

75. Groups that develop naturally in an organization without management having anything to do with it are called:

(A) industrial groups
(B) informal groups
(C) intensive groups
(D) social groups
(E) peer groups

76. People work harder or better to achieve goals that are (1)_____ rather than (2)_____.

(A) (1) specific, (2) general
(B) (1) accepted, (2) rejected
(C) (1) challenging, (2) easy
(D) all of the above
(E) none of the above

77. If a leader has power and influence because he is liked, admired and respected, he is said to have what KIND of power?

(A) legitimate
(B) reward
(C) coercive
(D) referent
(E) expert

78. Adaptive demands on individuals such as excessive heat or role conflicts are called:

(A) satisfiers
(B) motivators
(C) stress
(D) stressors
(E) sublimators

79. The typical behaviors expected of a job-holder are referred to by the term:

(A) job
(B) position
(C) role
(D) Type A personality
(E) group norms

80. The idea that once procedures are established, management should focus on those cases where standards are not being met is called the _____ principle:

(A) action
(B) exception
(C) emergency
(D) standards
(E) X-Y

81. The control process includes all BUT ONE of the following. Which is NOT included:

(A) measurable performance standards
(B) maximum performance possible
(C) measurement of performance
(D) feedback of information on deviation to management
(E) none of the above

82. To be effective, controls (and the feedback of control information) should have all of the following qualities EXCEPT:

(A) timely and relevant
(B) widely publicized
(C) desired and accepted by users
(D) descriptive and objective
(E) understandable to users

83. According to Douglas McGregor Theory X emphasizes (1)_____ controls while Theory Y emphasizes (2)_____ controls.

(A) (1) excessive, (2) inadequate
(B) (1) expensive, (2) inexpensive
(C) (1) tough, (2) weak
(D) (1) external, (2) self
(E) none of the above

84. In the graphic method of determining Economic Order Quantity, EOQ is the point at which:

(A) ordering costs exceed carrying costs
(B) total costs are lowest
(C) both of the above
(D) E=Q
(E) none of the above

85. The ABC Inventory System focuses attention on those groups of inventory items that are:

(A) most costly
(B) most numerous
(C) most critical to operations
(D) both A and C but NOT B
(E) none of the above

86. The use of upper and lower control limits on charts on which are plotted sample averages and ranges would be most associated with:

   (A) Economic Order Quantity
   (B) statistical process control
   (C) PERT
   (D) MRP II
   (E) WW II

87. A Gantt chart is useful for (and is primarily used for):

   (A) obtaining financial ratios
   (B) leverage analysis
   (C) scheduling
   (D) environmental forecasting
   (E) break-even analysis

88. The sequence of activities which requires the largest total time for its completion in a PERT chart is called the:

   (A) critical path
   (B) delta function
   (C) just-in-time method
   (D) PERTinent sequence
   (E) chart completion time

89. In a PERT or CPM network, activities are to events as:

   (A) a race is to the finish
   (B) a house is to a hammer
   (C) a horse is to the rider
   (D) time is to distance
   (E) bosses are to subordinates

90. A financial statement which shows assets, liabilities and stockholder's equity as of a particular date, is usually called a:

   (A) financial inventory
   (B) break-even table
   (C) income statement
   (D) activity ratio
   (E) none of the above

91. The income statement for a given year would provide which of the following?

   (A) revenue for the year (e.g., total sales)
   (B) cost of goods sold
   (C) total expenses
   (D) all of the above
   (E) none of the above

92. The item LEAST likely to be found in an operating budget is:

   (A) cost of new manufacturing machinery
   (B) wages of hourly workers
   (C) salaries of executives
   (D) heating expenses
   (E) sales revenues

93. When we know how to make a decision, what procedures to follow, and what information will be needed, the decision is said to be (1) _____ and is supported by (2) _____ systems.

   (A) (1) algebraic, (2) redundancy
   (B) (1) routine, (2) decision support
   (C) (1) structured, (2) (management) reporting systems
   (D) (1) unstructured, (2) decision support system
   (E) (1) superfluous, (2) computer

94. In a bank, the cashing of checks and handling of withdrawals and deposits would be processed by:

   (A) decision support systems
   (B) (management) reporting systems
   (C) transaction processing systems
   (D) first-line management systems
   (E) middle management systems

95. Western Bank Corporation's MIS processes deposit and withdrawal transactions and at the end of each day prints out a report of net increase or decrease in deposits compared to the previous day, month and year. In this example, deposits and withdrawals are:

   (A) elements
   (B) outcomes
   (C) data
   (D) data processing
   (E) information

96. Well known programming languages include:

   (A) BASIC, COBOL, FORTRAN
   (B) PROFAN, INCLO, TRANFOR
   (C) third generation, fifth generation, seventh generation
   (D) pre-user; transactor; end-user
   (E) none of the above

97. Programs of computer instructions that control the operations performed by the hardware of a computer system are called:

   (A) icons
   (B) archons
   (C) dedicated circuits
   (D) software
   (E) none of the above

98. An arithmetic logic unit, a control unit and a memory unit or component would most probably be found in (a, an):

   (A) software library
   (B) COBOL
   (C) central processing unit
   (D) input unit
   (E) PERT

99. Determining the mix or blend of fertilizer components that would best achieve some objective would be an appropriate application of:

   (A) layoff schedules
   (B) linear programming
   (C) queuing theory
   (D) economic order quantity
   (E) none of the above

100. Staff specialists in the use of quantitative methods for making management decisions are known as:

   (A) quantum managers
   (B) top management
   (C) line and staff methodologists
   (D) management scientists
   (E) staff managers

STOP

If you finish before the time limit is reached, you may check your work on this section only.

Answers To Sample Examination

1.   A   Planning is a management function focusing almost entirely on the future. B, C, D, and E are also management functions, but are concerned more with the present.

2.   B   The organizing function involves structuring of authority relationships. A, C, D, and E are functions that focus on other aspects of management.

3.   C   Staffing provides qualified people to fill the organizational structure.

4.   E   Controlling is concerned with insuring that performance conforms to plans.

5.   C   Plant managers supervise other managers and are in turn supervised by higher level management. A is at the top management level. B and D are first-line management.

6.   B   Mintzberg's categories are "interpersonal", "informational", and "decisional."

7.   B   F. W. Taylor is the "Father of Scientific Management." Frank and Lilian Gilbreth were among his associates.

            A are classical theorists. C are involved in founding the "human relations" movement or behavioral approach. D are sometimes called "neo-classical theorists"; they criticized both Scientific Management and classical theory. E— Drucker, is an eclectic writer not identified with any school.

8.   A   Fayol was the "father of modern management" and a recognized leader of the classical approach.

9.   D   Contingency approaches take the view that what is the best way to manage or to lead depends on the specifics of the situation.

10.   D   The Systems Approach emphasizes the interaction and interdependence of parts of the organization as well as transactions with the environment across organization boundaries.

11.   E   All of the above: governments, laws, customers and other organizations are included in the environment in which organizations operate.

12.   D   All of the above: an ethical decision ought to lead to a practicable or feasible course of action; it ought to consider profit since this is good for both owners and employees and is essential (at least in the long run) for organizational survival; what is socially acceptable should be considered although the most ethical course of action may sometimes not be acceptable to the majority of the public.

13.   C   Forms of international business include direct investment, portfolio investment (owning foreign stocks and bonds), joint venture, and the multi-national firm. Mediation and arbitration are forms of dispute resolution discussed under collective bargaining in Chapter Four: Staffing.

14.   D   Multi-national firm or multi-national corporation (MNF or MNC).

15.   C   The term global corporation is sometimes used to refer to an enterprise which makes and distributes a single product such as petroleum, cement, soft drinks (e.g., Coca-Cola) worldwide.

16.   D   The sequence of steps in planning includes: identify goals; find or develop alternative courses of action and choose one; develop operating objectives and supporting plans; review plans and the planning process.

17.   C   Strategic planning is a top management responsibility.

18.   B   The priority or sequence of development would be: 1) mission, 2) goal, 3) strategies, 4) operational objectives and plans.

19.   D   Standing plans include policies, procedures and rules. Budgets and projects are single-use plans.

20.   D   Policies guide decisions and thought. Rules specify what is to be done.

21.   B   A rolling plan is a plan covering a specified time period which is regularly updated and extended for the same period.

22.   A   The exception is control.

23.   B   Control involves determining whether actions and results have deviated from plans—hence plans are tools for the control process.

24.   A   Predicted enrollment. B refers to last year, hence is not a _forecast_. C is likewise not a forecast because it refers to the present. While D is a forecast it does not deal directly with sales or demand.

25.   D   A, B, and C have all been used for sales forecasting.

26.   C   Simon's three phases of decision-making are intelligence, design and choice.

27.   A   Almost all authorities recommend problem definition or understanding as the starting point.

28.   D   Payoff matrix. See discussion in text and Figure 2-2.

29.   D   A decision tree can be constructed to show the same information and contingent and expected values as a payoff matrix. See Figures 2-3A and 2-3B.

30.   A   Dollars. See Figures 2-4A and 2-4B. The quantity sold in units is usually shown on the horizontal axis.

31.   A   At the break-even point only A is true. If total revenues continue to increase and exceed total costs, the difference will be profit. C is not the break-even point since it is simply the definition of total costs and is true of all points on the total costs line.

32.   D   Span of control is the number of persons supervised by each supervisor.

33. E The principle is the exception principle. Thus the correct answer is E, "none of the above." The exception principle is viewed as an important concept for the control function.

34. D The scalar principle states that there should be a single clear and distinct line of authority or chain of command from the top of the organization to each position down through to the lowest levels.

35. C Functional authority—limited to the area of functional specialization. Presumably the personnel specialist reports to the Plant Manager who exercises line authority. The functional authority is part of the established authority relationships in the organization—it may even appear in writing—hence it is not informal.

36. D The exception. According to Weber, officials of a bureaucracy are selected on the basis of education, experience and competence, often established by examination.

37. A Unit and small batch was one of Woodward's technology types. The other two were assembly line (mass production) and continuous process.

38. C In contrast to traditional organizations which tend to operate on a one-on-one superior subordinate basis with responsibility individualized, Likert proposed that the organization should function as a system of groups held together by "linking pins"—persons who were members of two or more overlapping groups.

39. D Authority and responsibility should be equal. The person held responsible should be given enough authority to do the job. The person with the authority should be held responsible for the results.

40. D This is a good example of functional departmentation.

41. B Unity of command.

42. A A line relationship involves line authority over all those who are direct subordinates: line authority is the right to act and to command. Staff authority is limited to giving advice and recommendations. It may or may not be efficient. It usually is unambiguous.

43. C Chandler argued that changes in strategy led to changes in structure—therefore, when enterprises moved from a single-product business to a diversified group of business, the organizational structure changed from a centralized functional form to that of the decentralized firm consisting of product divisions (subsidiary companies).

44. B Knowledge and experience were assumed to be greatest at the top of the organizational pyramid—therefore, a justification for centralized decision-making.

45. C This is the definition of formalization.

46. E Complexity—another definition.

47. A   The more interdependence is required (for instance by technology) the greater the need to design the organizational structure so that it facilitates and enhances coordination.

48. C   Staffing. This is one definition.

49. B   EEO, initials for Equal Employment Opportunity. Such laws and regulations of the Equal Employment Opportunity Commissions (federal and state) would ordinarily be of prime concern to the Personnel Department.

50. D   Title VII bars employment discrimination based on race, color, religion, national origin and sex.

51. A   Personnel or Human Resources Department.

52. D   Job specification—lays out the education, experience skills and knowledge required to do the job.

53. D   Job evaluation. B and C are explained above. Performance appraisal describes how well a specific job occupant has performed.

54. C   Gantt charts are the exception—they are used in scheduling.

55. A   The interview—of which there are many kinds—is almost always part of the selection process.

56. D   All of the above. The compensation system must seem fair and be based on performance. You should not have to have a Ph.D. in econometrics to understand it.

57. D   OJT—on-the-job training, perhaps the oldest and most widely used training method.

58. C   The first step of most grievance procedures is an attempt to have the problem resolved by the grievant's immediate supervisor.

59. D   All of the things mentioned in A, B and C are uses for information about management employees.

60. B   The final step of the grievance procedure under most union contracts is compulsory arbitration in which both sides agree in advance to submit the grievance to an outside arbitrator and to abide by his decision.

61. B   Assessment centers are given generally good ratings by researchers as a valid selection method. They actually include a variety of methods including pencil-and-paper and performance activities. None of the other answers are selection procedures.

         Job posting is the announcement of a vacancy to the employees of an organization.

62. E   Needs assessment (analysis of the purpose of the program together with existing levels of knowledge and skill) should be done before any new training effort is started.

63.   C   Promotion-from-within policies are usually viewed favorably by employees, However, they limit the organization to its present employees as a source for filling positions at higher levels and this may exclude more competent candidates from outside.

64.   E   None of the above. Maslow's Need Hierarchy has five groups of needs (physiological, safety, love, esteem and self-actualization). Needs lower in the hierarchy have to be satisfied before higher needs can be active.

65.   E   None of the above. The assumptions are those of McGregor's "Theory Y."

66.   C   This describes a person with a high need for achievement.

67.   A   Herzberg's Motivator-Hygiene Theory led directly to what Herzberg now calls "orthodox" job enrichment—adding responsibilities and other "motivators" to the job to make it more challenging.

68.   A   Positive reinforcement—something desirable or satisfying that follows the behavior and makes its continuance more likely—in this case, a simple "thank you."

69.   A   Extinction (sometimes called omission) is the absence of any reinforcement following a behavior—when this happens the behavior gradually stops.

70.   A   In the expectancy model effort or motivation is the result of multiplying expectancy times instrumentality times valence ($E = E \times I \times V$).

71.   E   None of these. The trait approach is the one described.

72.   C   This is one definition of leadership.

73.   B   Contingency Theories assert that the most effective behavior is contingent (depends on) situational factors and/or factors in the leader himself/herself.

74.   C   Participative leadership gives subordinates the opportunity to participate in decisions.

75.   B   Informal groups develop for a variety of reasons without any action of management and despite opposition by management. Some informal groups are peer groups, but others are made up of people of different ranks or levels in the organization.

76.   D   All of the above are characteristics of effective goals.

77.   D   Referent power is based on liking, respect or admiration. A, B, C and D are other kinds of power.

78.   D   Stressors are the demands themselves, like physical injury or threat. The stressors result in a response or reaction called stress.

79.   C   Role is defined thus.

80. B The exception principle. Routine matters should be handled at lower levels; higher management should concern itself with unprogrammed decisions—the exceptional cases.

81. B Maximum performance possible is NOT part of the control process or even necessarily an advisable or planned outcome.

82. B "Widely publicized" is not necessarily a desirable or effective attribute. Typically criticism (a form of feedback control) is given in private.

83. D Theory X emphasizes external control while Theory Y relies on internal control or self-control.

84. B B is correct.

85. D Both A and C but NOT B. The ABC approach assigns to Category A, those materials whose control is most important (e.g., items most critical or most costly).

86. B Statistical process control. Sample means and ranges are plotted on a control chart—if they fall within the upper and lower control limits, the process is said to be "in control"; if not, it is "out of control."

87. C Gantt Charts are useful scheduling tools.

88. A The critical path is the sequence of activities in a PERT or CPM network which requires the greatest total amount of time for its completion.

89. A Events are the start or end of an activity. Events do not extend over time; activities do.

90. E None of the above. This is a description of a "balance sheet"—a financial control tool.

91. D An income statement would include total sales, cost of goods sold and total expenses thus yielding net profit or loss. Another financial control tool.

92. A Cost of machinery would appear in the capital budget NOT the operating budget.

93. C Management reporting systems (or simply, reporting systems) provide the information system support for structured (routine) decisions.

94. C Deposits, withdrawals, sales, etc., are transactions processed by the transaction processing system within the MIS.

95. C The transactions (deposits, withdrawals) are data.

    The report of net increase or decrease is information.

96. A All of these are programming languages.

97. D Software programs provide instructions to the computer system.

98.   C   Components of the central processing unit (CPU) of a computer include arithmetic logic, control and memory units.

99.   B   This is an appropriate use for linear programming.

100. D   Management scientists specialize in the application of quantitative methods to the analysis and solution of management problems.

NOTES

NOTES

NOTES

NOTES

NOTES